BILL FERRIS is regarded as one of the fathers of the venture capital industry in Australia. He formed the country's first venture capital company in 1970, having studied the emerging sector in the United States while completing his MBA at the Harvard Business School.

Bill Ferris teamed up in 1987 with a friend, Joseph Skrzynski, to form Australian Mezzanine Investments Pty Limited (AMIL), a venture capital funds manager. AMIL has continued to perform as one of the outstanding successes in the now rapidly expanding venture capital sector of Australia. Its investments in companies such as Datacraft, Austal Ships, Cuppa Cup Vineyards, LookSmart, Fingerscan and many others have yielded high returns to the AMIL funds' investors. These investments have also created more than 50 millionaire entrepreneurs and executives in the process, as well as helping to create many thousands of jobs around the country.

Bill Ferris has been chairman of both the Australian Trade Commission and the Australian Venture Capital Association and in 1990 was made an Officer of the Order of Australia for services to the export industry. Bill is now chairman of the Asia Pacific Council of Macquarie University and a director of the Australian Institute of Management. He is actively involved in the venture capital industry as executive chairman of Australian Mezzanine Investments Pty Limited.

nothing ventured, nothing gained

Thrills and spills in venture capital

BILL FERRIS

ALLEN & UNWIN

First published in 2000 by
Allen & Unwin
9 Atchison Street
St Leonards NSW 1590
Australia
Phone: (61 2) 8425 0100
Fax: (61 2) 9906 2218
Email: frontdesk@allen-unwin.com.au
Web: http://www.allen-unwin.com.au

National Library of Australia
Cataloguing-in-Publication entry:

Ferris, W.D.
Nothing ventured, nothing gained: thrills and spills in venture capital.

Includes index.
ISBN 1 86508 281 3.

1. Australian Mezzanine Investments Pty Ltd. 2. Small business investment companies—Australia. 3. Venture capital—Australia.
I. Title.

332.67220994

Set in 11/13.5 pt Janson by DOCUPRO, Sydney
Printed by Griffin Press Pty Ltd, Adelaide

TO MY PARENTS

contents

Part two

acknowledgements

The writing of this book was made possible by taking 'sabbatical' leave from my Australian Mezzanine Investment responsibilities midway through 1999. This three and a half months' absence from the office placed an increased load on friends and colleagues, and I wish to thank, in particular, my partners Joe Skrzynski, Su-Ming Wong, Andrew Savage and Paul Riley for shouldering most of the extra burden.

My assistant Cynthia Waters has battled with the manuscript over many months to make it possible to present a satisfactory disk to the publisher on time. And I owe much to the research efforts of my colleagues and friends Karen Markell and Darren Smorgon.

As usual, all errors, omissions and shortcomings rest squarely with the author.

W.D. Ferris
December 1999

introduction

Since founding Australia's first venture capital company in 1970, I have been enamoured with the sector, with what it stands for and what it has and will achieve. Since those early days, the venture capital sector has grown in fits and starts, in recent years maturing into a well-organised and significant segment of the capital markets with more than $3 billion presently under management. In the financial year 1998/99 alone almost $700 million was invested by venture capitalists in a range of unlisted companies across the country.

During the past twelve years, the venture capital activities of my firm Australian Mezzanine Investments Pty Limited (AMIL) have assisted in the creation of more than 50 millionaires throughout the country. We have also played a role in the creation of many thousands of jobs and the generation of hundreds of millions of dollars in exports and taxes. We have enjoyed many wins and some losses. Always interesting and often exhilarating for those of us involved, the venture capital business is quite different from any other capital investing activity. Yet this venture capital process has rarely been analysed as have the other segments of the capital markets.

What is venture capital? As the name implies, it is capital ventured by investors willing to take, and capable of taking, the risks associated with young and rapidly expanding businesses. Venture capital is provided by professionally staffed and managed venture capital funds which typically take an equity (a shareholding) position in their 'investees', the entrepreneurial companies. This form of investing clearly differs from that of banks and other institutions, which lend their funds and expect their clients to return the loans with interest. In terms of security, lenders rank ahead of the shareholders; in the event that a company is unsuccessful the lender may still recover all or most of its loan, but the venture capital equity investor is likely to lose all. Venture capital is thus the essential risk capital required by entrepreneurs seeking to start new companies, expand existing businesses or try out new technologies or products.

The major suppliers of venture capital are the large Australian superannuation funds, which nowadays allocate up to 5 per cent of their total assets to this riskier class of investment. The big super funds typically invite specialist venture capital management companies, like Australian Mezzanine Investments Pty Limited, to manage their allocations to this relatively difficult and hands-on investment area. In return for the extra risk these investors expect to earn above average returns, not less than 5 per cent above what they might expect from simply investing in listed stock exchange securities.

The venture capital process is a quintessential blend of art and science in commerce. It is *art* in that it involves judgement of people (the entrepreneurs and their team executives), along with assessment of their integrity, their drive, their thirst for financial and product success. And it is art also in the sense of timing—is the tide of economic and other events right for this innovation or is the whole project premature, such that we will find ourselves swimming against an ebbing flow?

It is *science* in the sense of analysing what it is that is truly distinctive and competitive about each project. Is there innovation in product or service? If so, is it sustainable and, in any case, will consumers pay for the difference? And what else is coming out of the laboratories in California or Tel Aviv or Perth that can blow this apparent competitive advantage away?

Thus venture capitalists have to be both artist and scientist. Once they have made an investment, the other two ingredients required during the life of the investment are hard work and a measure of luck.

The venture capitalist will normally require a seat on the board of directors of each investee company. This enables the investor to closely monitor the operating performance of the business and, importantly, to contribute as an involved partner to the actions of that business. The venture capitalist will often act as an objective sounding board for the entrepreneur chief executive on issues such as salary levels, recruitment of key personnel, strategy development and so on. This can sometimes simply take the form of good listening and hand-holding skills on a range of issues which the CEO may feel are too sensitive or inappropriate for discussion with his or her own employees. At other times it will involve the venture capitalist in a detailed understanding and analysis of the company's strengths and weaknesses, of acquisition and divestiture opportunities. The venture capitalist may arrange a refinancing, and may often ultimately find a buyer for the business. The venture capital investor may also occasionally need to step in to run the company, replacing an underperforming chief executive. The venture capitalist's role is obviously a very hands-on one from time to time during the life of each investment.

In my experience, throughout 30 years as a practising venture capitalist, hard work helps to avoid losses but luck is probably more important in generating truly exceptional profits. The stories that make up Part One of the book illustrate this experience and perhaps provide a guide for others seeking to enter the world of professional venture capital.

In these case descriptions I make repeated reference to three key components of investment analysis that venture capitalists typically focus on:

- Core proposition: What is the core proposition of the deal? Why can we expect to make exceptional returns from this investment? What is so different or superior about this product or service that ensures above average profits and a sustainable competitive position? Is there protectable intellectual property? (Each core proposition must be capable of articulation in less than one page.)

- KEY PEOPLE: Who are the key executives that will make all this happen? Do they have their lives on the line for this? What experience, contacts and existing business opportunities do they bring to the table? Are they people of integrity?
- NUMBERS: What do the numbers look like and are they credible? If the core proposition is exciting and the people check out, just how good are the numbers anyway? If everything goes to plan, what are the likely financial returns? And how disastrous will they be if things go badly? How do these various upside and downside cases or scenarios correlate with the nature of the risks involved? In other words, does the risk/reward profile really warrant the exposure of time and money?

In the following case descriptions, each of these three components are examined with the clinical benefit of hindsight. Success or failure can usually be sheeted home to the degree to which the pre-analysis of the critical components actually applied in practice—always acknowledging that luck invariably plays a key role too, sometimes wonderfully and sometimes horribly. In every case, nothing ventured, nothing gained.

In Part Two of the book, I review the development of the venture capital sector in Australia and give a short account of my own company.

part ONE

I am on the deck of a 16.5 metre Robert Ladd–designed ketch, sailing down the coast of Turkey with my wife. The crew has just served us an aubergine and lemon salad with a side dish of yoghurt and olives. We are washing this down with a cool Bordeaux. The temperature is 27°C, the wind is from the north at about 15 knots apparent and we are making 7 or 8 knots, heading from Bodrum down to Simi. Indeed, we are hoping to arrive in time for dinner on that beautiful island, which used to boast the world's premier shipbuilding industry in the days when the ancient Greeks were all-conquering.

In fact I am part way through a well-earned sabbatical: three months of relaxation and exploration, together with work on this book.

After 30 years in the venture capital business I had begun to wonder whether my investing experiences, successful and unsuccessful, would be interesting and even instructive for others, especially those contemplating a career in this most exciting and creative segment of the capitalist system. Finally I decided they might be.

So, let me take you now on a sort of picaresque journey replete with venture capital adventures. Hopefully, the stories will convey various lessons, some amusing and others sobering. For reasons that will become clear, in a few cases the names of individuals and companies are codenames.

some deals that went badly wrong

Associated Bitumen Sprayers Pty Ltd

It seems so long ago—an investment in the early seventies—but it offers some wonderful lessons in what not to do. I can't remember the exact amount of money involved—about $200 000—but I do remember that we lost the lot! And in fairly quick time, too.

I had just returned to Australia in 1970 having obtained my

MBA from the Harvard Business School. I had become fascinated by the venture business in the United States and had decided to start my own, and Australia's first, venture capital company. I remember receiving lots of advice (in retrospect, I now realise, very good advice) from people such as Rod Carnegie and Bryan Kelman, who said that I should work for a US venture firm for some years prior to starting an enterprise of that sort in Australia. Sir Roderick was then head of McKinsey's practice in Australia and later the chairman of CRA; Bryan ran CSR's concrete and quarrying businesses and subsequently became CEO of the overall group.

I was 25 years of age, impatient and genuinely fearful that if I did not then launch out on my own I would never do so. I feared that I would go to Wall Street and never emerge from that wondrous jungle. I decided to return to Australia since the prospect of pioneering venture capital in my own country was irresistible: perhaps it was a case of heart over head.

From my pre-Harvard days of working as Bryan Kelman's assistant at CSR, I knew a bit about the road aggregates contracting business.

Peter Nagle had been referred to me by someone in the industry and he presented me with his plan to commence a 'renegade' road aggregates and bitumen spraying business in New South Wales and in Fiji. Why Fiji, you ask? Well, I will come to that soon.

The road surfacing business in those days 'belonged' to just a few companies: Boral, Shell, Mobil and Blue Metal Industries (BMI). There was no Australian Competition and Consumer Commission in those days, otherwise its chairman Alan Fels would have had them all for lunch, so widespread and blatant were the arrangements for geographic sharing and pricing. These circumstances made it interesting for a renegade operator to enter the market.

Peter Nagle's business proposition was as follows. His new company, Associated Bitumen Sprayers (ABS), would bid on New South Wales country town road contracts at prices approximately 20 per cent below the majors. ABS would win some of these and complete them profitably, given its much lower overhead cost structure; it would then threaten to enter the big city markets where the majors made most of their monopolistic profits. Nagle's CORE PROPOSITION was that not only would the majors be unable to meet ABS's prices on contracts bid by ABS, but they would have to drop their prices on *all* tenders. Otherwise ABS would easily win a predatory pricing action in the courts and the majors would be fined big time and suffer public humiliation to boot.

Thus ABS's entry might well cost the industry 20 per cent across the board—many millions of dollars each year. The idea was to cause enough havoc that one or other of the majors would bid to take over ABS at a massive profit to Nagle and his financial partners.

I was attracted to this core proposition. In my concrete and quarrying days, I had seen similar successful sorties with entrepreneurs enjoying takeouts by big ready-mix concrete groups like CSR, BMI, Boral and Pioneer. Each of these corporations had invested heavily in the infrastructure of quarries, crushing plants and fleets of delivery vehicles. Steady pricing was critical to the bottom line; an upstart operator with a secondhand truck and a source of river gravel and sand could cause havoc. Such upstarts were invariably run out or bought out. I had participated on the heavyweight side of this game and had seen some of the renegade operators' profits at first hand.

The ABS game plan fitted this experience. In other words, I was happy that the core proposition made sense.

Next, checking the KEY PEOPLE. Nagle had worked as a fairly senior sales executive with one of the major oil companies. He therefore had a reasonably good knowledge of the industry players and dynamics—the 'mud map', if you will. We had satisfactory industry references although, when I now look back on the checking process, there's no way that Peter could get through our screening today. He had no track record of money making; he was a sales guy, not an operations executive; and we were aware of reports of alcohol abuse in years gone by. But leopards can change their spots, can't they?

At least we had enough sense to immediately supplement the management team in the New South Wales business with a competent young financial accountant.

Turning to the third component of the venture capitalist's

trilogy, the NUMBERS looked pretty good. It was a high risk game plan requiring enough firepower to seriously take on the majors for at least a couple of years until a takeover offer might be forthcoming. The upside case reasonably suggested three times our money back in two years and maybe a lot more if we could cause enough damage to the market.

What happened? It was a great, swashbuckling adventure. ABS won several tenders and managed to break even on most of them. This was in spite of the efforts of the majors to bully some of the suppliers into delaying deliveries to ABS. These efforts reached farcical proportions when one morning ABS found all its spraying equipment vehicles with flat tyres, including the foreman's utility.

Well into the second year it was clear that our CEO was not an operations man. Costs were uncontrolled, tenders were badly priced, manhours never properly measured and so on. We were still burning cash at about $10 000 per month. The company had leased most of its equipment and we had invested about $150 000 in cash as the 'firepower' working capital needed to sustain the campaign.

I calculated that ABS had maybe another 60 days before it ran out of cash. Still no takeover offer in sight. Through the trade press, Nagle announced ABS's ambitions to expand its activities into the metropolitan centres of Sydney and Melbourne and a joint venture with a CSR subsidiary for similar activities in Fiji. Still no response from anyone! So, at fifteen days before D-day my good friend and co-director at the time, Rodney O'Neil (from the famous O'Neil Hymix concrete empire), rang Sir Elton Griffin to make an appointment for me to visit.

Sir Elton had a formidable reputation in Australian business circles as a tough, driving bull of a man. He had breathed life and then fire into Boral, building it entrepreneurially into a well-respected industrial enterprise across Australia. Sir Elton was a hands-on, no-nonsense operations man. He was not an MBA yuppie like me. His office was austere and, from memory, rather bare. He sat on his side of a large desk and leered down at Rodney O'Neil and me in our lower seats. His eyes fixed discerningly on me and seemed to anticipate my words even before I uttered them.

Nonetheless, he gave me a fair hearing as I explained the wonderful opportunity ABS had in Fiji and that we were presently weighing up whether to invest more heavily into the New South Wales business or move everything into Fiji. I thought that given his experience, etc, he might have some advice, some ideas . . .

Sir Elton smiled at Rodney and then at me, leaned right across his desk, pumping his right-hand index finger up and down on an imaginary spray can, and said, 'Do you know what this is? . . . psst, psst, it's a bloody Mortein payment. I'll pay you $100 000 to get rid of you insects out of this business . . . psst, psst, take it or leave it, here and now.'

Needless to say, we tried over the next few days to negotiate a better payment, but Sir Elton was true to his word. We accepted the Mortein payment, Boral took over the equipment and ABS never made another spray in Australia.

ABS now had all of its cash back, but no profits, only bruises to show for its trouble.

During this time Nagle had been approached by a former Mobil colleague, now working for Mobil in Fiji, to consider entering the asphalt spraying business in that tropical paradise. Fiji was opening up with a major thrust on tourism in a frantic bid to compensate for the decline of the sugar industry. In the sixties, the aptly named and wonderfully imperial Colonial Sugar Refining Company Limited (now more modestly badged CSR Limited) had announced its intention to withdraw from the sugar business in Fiji. CSR was the largest employer in that country and had made a spectacular and positive impact on the economy over many decades. It had not been an easy decision for the company, emotionally or politically, but one which commercially could no longer be ignored. The end of an era had come when one of the greatest plantation owner/developer models of all time had run its course.

In the exit transition, CSR very responsibly set out to find other economic activities that it might stimulate in the Fijian economy; that is, activities about which it had some direct knowledge in Australia, for example concrete and quarrying. In the early seventies, a joint venture in quarrying was established between CSR and a local Indian operator, Sethi Narain. Mr Narain operated the only two licensed quarries on the island, one on the Nadi side and the other on the Suva side. Both quarries were ideally situated close to the developing markets for road and concrete aggregates and both were monopoly supply situations. In short, they were licences to print money, weren't they?

My early boss at CSR, Bryan Kelman, confirmed that Nagle had been chatting to Narain about extending the joint venture's quarrying activities into bitumen spraying. CSR had really only been acting as a catalyst to get this enterprise up and going in Fiji and did not see it as a long-term strategic fit, given its overall withdrawal strategy. And so it was that ABS was presented with an opportunity to join as a shareholder in the Fijian company operating in quarrying, ready-mixed concrete and asphalting services. ABS would provide approximately $200 000 for asphalting equipment and would manage the operations.

During my apprenticeship years with CSR between 1962 and 1966, I had the good fortune of visiting Fiji on a number of occasions. My task was to learn from and 'keep an eye on' the company's special quarry consultant, Arthur Harrison. I should give Arthur his proper title: Group Captain Arthur Harrison. Arthur had been a fighter pilot based in Darwin during the war years, had no love for the Japanese, great love for a gin and tonic and an insatiable love for anything in a skirt. He was a very handsome, upright roué in his early sixties. He would swan into CSR's senior executive floor on O'Connell Street in a seersucker suit with a red carnation in the button hole. Bryan Kelman was his patron and so he got away with this behaviour, even at a time when Colonial Sugar did not hire Jews or Catholics, when only men were allowed to smoke and when an old school tie was not just a help but de rigeur.

I remember Arthur was always positive, always fun, and his feasibility studies were always sound. That was why Kelman kept him around. Kelman had an extraordinary ability to work with all sorts of personalities, to get the very best out of them, and usually to have fun doing so.

So, to get back to Fiji, Arthur had previously shown me the Narain quarries, had analysed the quantity and quality of the reserves and was convinced of their commercial viability. He still found time to show me every bar and nightspot worthy of a group captain on both sides of the island.

We decided to take the Fijian plunge and our hero, Peter Nagle, eagerly relocated to Suva.

At this stage, I married my first and only wife, Lea, and I arranged for the tail end of our honeymoon to be in Fiji. I had apparently overlooked telling Lea about our prospective business venture in Fiji and the need for me to hold one or two meetings while we were there. This omission, plus a large helping of *kava* which she obligingly consumed when visiting our new partners at the Suva quarry, created a cocktail of tears and illness for the balance of our honeymoon. It turned out that she was also pregnant at the time—come to think of it, that may be why our son Ben is now teaching Greek and Latin instead of becoming a venture capitalist.

Perhaps the more important meetings were in the offices of our Indian partner, Sethi Narain. Sethi was a sophisticated, successful and quite charming man in his early forties. His grandfather had arrived from India as an indentured labourer sometime in the nineteenth century. The indigenous Fijians did not choose to cut cane in the blazing heat; curiously they preferred to swim, catch fish, lie around and basically have a healthy good time. So something like 20 000 Indian slave labourers were 'temporarily imported' into the country to work the sugar plantations. These 'temporary' inhabitants stayed and multiplied and today outnumber the native Fijian population. Sethi's family had prospered in a variety of trading activities and had shown vision and dexterity in securing the monopoly stone supply position.

Sethi's finance director was a young man with twelve fingers—more specifically, eight fingers and four thumbs. During our discussions, he would constantly stroke the smaller of his thumbs. I found that whenever I spoke to him I actually addressed his thumbs. I simply could not take my eyes off them, hard as I tried. I am sure you have had a similar experience when, try as you might, you cannot take your eyes off someone's eccentric habit or marking.

Peter and I, in the grand Australian tradition, came to give this fellow a fetching nickname: Thumbs Down. This proved entirely appropriate over the next two years. Not only did he have more thumbs to point down than any other man I've met, he also gave us the thumbs-down on any request for better trading terms from Sethi's trucking contractors, for better dividends or, frankly, for anything.

So what happened? The company did win tenders from the Suva City Council, but at prices well negotiated by the British and Australian advisors to the bureaucracy. Nagle's operating skills were certainly no stronger in Fiji than they had been in New South Wales. Plant breakdowns were numerous and, unlike in Australia, repairs took unfathomably long and were rarely complete. Parts and mechanics were equally scarce.

First year losses were unwelcome, but as Thumbs Down said to the board, 'What could you expect?' Year two losses deepened our problems. Our man Nagle's drinking problems had apparently re-emerged and, on one visit to Fiji, we eventually located him unconscious in the Suva gaol. It transpired that Nagle had instructed the company's oil broker to pay 15 per cent 'commissions' on all oil purchases into a special account, a very special Peter Nagle account. He subsequently told police that this was a 'bridging arrangement' only and had enabled him to settle some personal debts and the money would of course be repaid, etc, etc.

This 'bridging arrangement' grossly exacerbated the company's cash flow problems, and the game was up unless more cash was injected into the business. We had no more cash, CSR had no further appetite for this non-core activity, our entrepreneur was bankrupt and in the Suva gaol, and Thumbs Down gave the thumbs-up to the liquidator by purchasing all the assets for a nominal consideration that cleared out the remaining trade creditors.

So there it is. We lost the lot from this 'no-brainer'. The lessons are no doubt obvious, but let me summarise what the key ones were for me.

Lesson one *Having high profile shareholders/partners doesn't necessarily make a deal a good one.* They can and may help, but overreliance on the strength and credibility of such partners can bring you undone. I knew that the project was weak in terms of executive skills, but I thought the strength of the core proposition and the calibre of the partners would combine to make it work. This was sloppy thinking.

Lesson two *Leopards don't often change their spots.* Our leopard was always and only a salesman, not an operations executive. We expected him to do an operations job. This was at best naïve on my part and at worst unfair to everyone. No doubt Nagle's reversion to alcohol abuse was in part a direct outcome of this misfit between the job at hand and the skills in place.

Lesson three *A venture capitalist's returns are sometimes inversely proportional to the distance between his office and the investee company's office.* Fiji is a great place for a venture capitalist's first honeymoon, but not for his first deal.

Rumentek Industries Pty Ltd

For some years I had read and known a little about the Rumentek technology developed by the CSIRO. Ruminants—animals like cattle and sheep—have digestive mechanisms with multiple stomachs that enable them to eat and live the way they do without requiring bucket loads of alka seltzer each day. A cow has four rumens (stomachs): the first stomach is a massive bacterial chamber that gets rid of much of what comes in directly out the back door without any opportunity for meat or milk conversion. For example, anything higher than about 5 per cent fat intake is toxic to the animal and is rejected by the first stomach—or otherwise proves fatal.

Have I lost you? In retrospect, I would have been less poor and had fewer grey hairs if I had given up at this point also. But sometimes venture capitalists cannot help themselves. You see, the CSIRO had come up with a patented process for feeding animal supplements in a way that bypassed the animal's first and grossly inefficient stomach, allowing the supplements to be digested by the fourth stomach where immediate conversion to meat and milk occurs. So what? Well, if it worked, this could change the entire cattle feeding paradigm in Australia and worldwide, that's what!

The CORE PROPOSITION was that the technology enabled a 15 per cent better feed conversion, so providing enhanced economics for the commercial cattle feedlot industry. Furthermore, in one particular application, the Rumentek process allowed the production of healthier meat and milk. Feed supplements low in saturated fats, for example canola-based supplements, could bypass the first stomach and result in low-fat meat and milk production—low cholesterol foods naturally produced by the animal itself.

Extensive laboratory and field trials had been conducted by the CSIRO and the Rumentek company over several years and the results appeared very convincing, if still preliminary. The Rumentek company had a pilot feed production plant in Moree, close to the supply of requisite raw materials such as cottonseed. The company had negotiated worldwide rights to the CSIRO process and if the economics worked in Australia then markets such as the United States should also prove attractive.

The veracity of the proposition depended on assumptions about alternative feeding regimes and commodity prices and about the future direction of the cattle feedlot business in Australia and elsewhere. Assumptions about the important export markets of Japan and Korea were also key factors in the analysis. Lots of variables, lots of risks—in the technology, in the production economics, in the markets.

Nonetheless, in mid-1994 a colleague at Australian Mezzanine, Paul Riley, and I reckoned that this was a most exciting new technology project and we were convinced that the upside was truly exceptional. This was a world class project. We accepted that the downside could be a total wipeout—in this assessment we were to be proved remarkably accurate, as I will show.

But first, what about the KEY PEOPLE? The CSIRO scientist inventors, John Ashes and Trevor Scott, were and are very impressive men. Trevor joined the board of Rumentek and was passionate in his belief in and hopes for the process. Recognised worldwide as a leader in the science of animal nutrition, Trevor was fundamental to our belief in the veracity of the science. And, as it transpired, the low saturated fat claims for the process are now undeniably proven. In that respect, the scientists have been vindicated.

The real commercial leadership in Rumentek came from a mercurial animal nutritionist whom I will codename Micawber, after the famous optimist in Charles Dickens' *David Copperfield.* Micawber and his father had some prior and unprofitable experience using the CSIRO process to produce lamb for the Japanese market—but the meat smelt more like fish than lamb. It turns out that the Japanese don't like the smell of lamb. Micawber was successful in using the Rumentek process to remove the smell, but the margin wasn't there. The project turned out to be 'on the nose' for the investors and the company went into bankruptcy.

Micawber was a high energy man, entrepreneurial and a workaholic. It took us a year or two to realise that his optimism ran way ahead of actual results. Worse still, Micawber genuinely believed his own BS. He liked to see himself as a scientist, yet his scientific method was one that always selectively fitted the 'facts' to his preferred outcome. I do not believe this was ever other than unwitting on his part, but I stress the experience because it was a salutary one for all of us. When you want something so badly, you can rationalise all sorts of facts and figures; this was Micawber all over!

Early positive results masked this process of self-delusion. The number of cattle on Rumentek feed accelerated from about 10 000 at the time of investment to more than 30 000 within 18 months—right on business plan. This appeared to justify our initial $3 million investment in plant and equipment and accelerated our approval of the second $3 million tranche to fund subsequent working capital requirements.

Micawber's (and others') interpretation of these early commercial trials were very upbeat; subsequent analysis by the clients proved that the costs of the process exceeded the benefits derived.

Apart from Trevor Scott, to whom I referred above, three other key executive directors were involved. Ian Reid, a successful cattle breeder and farmer (and part beneficiary of the Reid family fortune), was a strong financial supporter and friend of the company. John Macphillamy had been infected by Micawber's optimism and was a live and active carrier. Macphillamy was responsible for the finances of the group—as it turned out he was better at raising it than at spending it. Still, all of us were guilty of that attribute in this particular venture.

Finally, there was Dr Doom, aka George Karhan. George was well known to me as a fellow member of the Young Presidents Organization. This is a US-based non-profit body formed to provide a unique opportunity for 'education through idea exchange' among young chief executives. CEOs must be under 40 years of age, running businesses of a certain minimum size in terms of sales and employees. The organisation has proved to be a very effective one for its members and has expanded around the world. In Australia there are now active chapters in Sydney, Melbourne, Perth, Adelaide and Brisbane.

George has successfully built and run his own plastics injection machinery business and has also been an astute investor from time to time in companies such as Memtec, when it was starting out in life. He had money in Rumentek and, while a great believer early on, he grew increasingly sceptical of Micawber's claims, so earning the title of Dr Doom. A man of integrity and wry, self-deprecating humour, he remains a director of the company today.

I must also mention a young man who, in 1997, was appointed general manager, charged with a brief to redirect the company and attempt to salvage value. Aged 26, Stirling McGregor comes from a distinguished and experienced pastoral family. He put some fresh money on the line and introduced a hardnosed approach to the difficult task of stemming the cash hæmorrhage running at about \$30 000 per month.

By the time McGregor got his hands on the reins, the damage to the company's reputation and to its resources were such that a turnaround would very likely prove elusive. This effort is still in progress, but in the meantime we have written off more than \$6 million!

How did experienced venture capitalists like us get into such a mess with this project? Let me stick to my format and describe the basic NUMBERS before dealing with this painful question.

Over a period of more than a decade prior to our involvement, not less than $20 million had been spent by the CSIRO and two research and development syndicates. This investment had facilitated the fundamental R&D, the early laboratory and field trials and the costs of a worldwide patenting process.

The Rumentek entrepreneurs had already invested about $1 million of their own money when we committed to a $3 million first mortgage loan to build a new plant; we also conditionally committed another $3 million equity for working capital. For this we acquired a 50 per cent interest in the Rumentek company and its intellectual property. Sales volume was an annual $1.5 million prior to our investment, rose to about $5 million in Year 3, and has since collapsed.

The company has been reconfigured and recapitalised, and in return for our forgiveness of debt—a fancy term used in financial circles and meaning a debt writeoff—we retain a 25 per cent equity interest in the company, going forward. Given that we have dropped more than $6 million down this agribusiness hole, what went wrong and what are the important lessons?

Lesson one Our analysis of the core proposition was flawed in one important regard. We allowed ourselves to be overly impressed by the science and spent too little time on the marketplace analysis. In fact, what we had was a solution looking for a problem—rather like the laser beam technology which sent so many people broke in the sixties and seventies before the market was ready for laser-based solutions. Beware of solutions looking for problems!

To be kind to all the Rumentek players, no one could have predicted the collapse that occurred in the cattle industry, in particular in the feedlot business. Prices dropped, export markets dried up, oversupply of cattle in the United States led to further pressure in the Japanese market, and drought conditions in northern New South Wales added to the woe. Clients who had previously been open to experimentation and field trials could no longer afford such risks and distractions. They were concentrating on downsizing and survival.

Furthermore, when we proved to the major retailers such as Coles Myer that Rumentek beef, milk and cheese were lower in saturated fats, they said, 'We like that but we cannot pay you any premium; oh, and we want you to pay for the promotion costs as well.' Until and unless there is a sufficient consumer pull for this sort of healthy product, our Rumentek solution will not be commercially viable.

So I guess the first lesson is: *Be sure your inventor's solution is solving a problem that the marketplace will pay for now, not in ten years' time.*

Lesson two A related lesson is: *Know when to stop flogging a dead horse*—or in this case a dead cow. Have the courage to call it quits.

Perhaps a more elegant and useful expression of this maxim is to insist on specific deliverable milestones against which to incrementally invest in these kinds of high risk projects. We fell into the trap of approving too much money too soon, based on over-dependence on apparent company results that were in fact not repeatable and sustainable in the marketplace.

Hindsight is a convenient lens with which to magnify the entrails one originally read, but how much better we and indeed the project would have been had we required more disciplined and objective outcomes for our first $3 million tranche. We should also have insisted that the company invite other investors at that point, rather than our chasing the original investment so aggressively. Easy in retrospect isn't it?

Lesson three Another lesson is this: *Never let a pathological optimist be the CEO.*

Entrepreneurs and venture capitalists need to be optimists, otherwise they would never get up in the morning. But I am referring to the likes of Mr Micawber who suffer self-delusion, who fit the facts to the outcome they so desperately want for you and themselves. Pathological optimists actually believe that what they are telling you is true and deliverable. These people are dangerous to themselves and everyone else around.

Lesson two is actually the most important one for me, going forwards. Of course, I hope to identify the Micawbers in future but, even if I don't, a rigorous regime of incremental investment, with drawdowns conditional upon clearly agreed project milestones, will better protect all concerned.

William Shakespeare must have foreseen my fate with Rumentek when he wrote in *Julius Cæsar*:

> There is a tide in the affairs of men,
> Which, taken at the flood, leads on to fortune;
> Omitted, all the voyage of their life
> Is bound in shallows and in miseries.

Specialty Jewellery Australia Pty Ltd

Diamonds may be a girl's best friend, but the retailer Specialty Jewellery Australia (SJA), turned out not to be one of ours!

SJA, in fact, began life as a chain of small stores selling relatively inexpensive gold jewellery to a young female market. The company was brought to our attention early in 1988 by a very old friend of mine, an incomparable networker, the unique anything-but-shy character, John Walton. Himself a retailer from the business empire started by his father, John had been mightily impressed by the performance of the SJA business and was keen to introduce the CEO to me.

John reminded me that back in 1970 I had interrupted him in the middle of a shower to secure his signature on a commitment to my very first venture fund. His introductory fee for the SJA deal would turn out to be three times the amount of his 1970 investment! With this fee negotiation out of the way, John introduced us to the SJA players: the CEO Howard Previn, the accountant Andrew Allbright, and the chief jewellery buyer John Pope (all three players, as well as the company, are codenamed).

Previn explained how his company had grown rapidly to now being a chain of 25 jewellery stores, each averaging sales of $1 million per annum. This growth had come partly at the expense of established competitors and partly, in Previn's view, through SJA's creation of new demand in the young female market.

The CORE PROPOSITION was as follows: SJA's small store retail format could be rolled out nationally, allowing economies of scale in terms of television advertising spend and in terms of the top management overheads. Pitching directly at the 16–30-year-old female office and factory worker, SJA would continue to expand its market share in this niche by dedicated product ranging and by a price discounting strategy that consolidated its position as the 'best value' jewellery retailer in the country. Furthermore, SJA's growth would be fuelled by its demonstrated ability to create new demand.

The average purchase at SJA was $100 and Previn believed that the competitors for his customers' discretionary dollars were not just the jewellery stores like Angus & Coote and Prouds but all the clothing boutiques as well. This was his opportunity to convince the young female to treat herself to $100 worth of jewellery rather than to a new skirt or blouse. Previn would roll out new stores in key shopping centres across the country and also identify acquisitions to accelerate the company's growth path towards a public listing.

If the people and the numbers stacked up, we agreed that this was a reasonable core proposition, given that the team had already successfully progressed from one store to 25 stores in the space of three years. How could you go wrong!? . . . Read on.

Of the KEY PEOPLE, Previn was the main author and proponent of the core proposition. He was key to the aggressive store rollout strategy. Previn and his leading jewellery maker, Ben Isaacs, and a marketing executive, David Faber, had all emigrated from South Africa five years earlier. Previn had been a chartered accountant in South Africa and had managed to get some of his funds out of the country with which to start the SJA business. He seemed hungry to build a successful business, but clearly did not have previous experience in managing a large number of employees in multiple locations. Nonetheless, he was tenacious and competent and our references checked out satisfactorily.

During the early growth phase of his company, Previn had

met up with an importer/wholesaler who was also the owner of a display case and retail fitout business. This was the pipe-smoking, mercurial John Pope. A lean Protestant from the northern suburbs of Sydney, Pope was a quite different personality from the two South African Jewish founders of SJA and from the tubby Catholic accountant, Andrew Allbright. Come to think of it, we had quite an ecumenical team on our hands!

Pope had sold his shop fittings business into SJA and continued to design and supply all of SJA's store fitouts. Equipment was also sold to other retailers. From the start, Pope struck us as always having a highly inflated view of the value of SJA and, in particular, of his personal contribution to that value. During our deal structuring discussions, he quickly adopted 'take it or leave it' positions. He would fix you with a steely glare, suck on his pipe and wait for you to say something. I think Pope was a believer in the negotiation principle that says you should listen rather than talk and never be embarrassed by silences.

Subsequently, Pope inserted and asserted himself into the senior position on the 'buy side' of the business. This was a fundamentally important position, sourcing gold, diamonds and other such materials and components for the company.

For all his eccentricity and prickliness, we concluded that Pope had been a reasonably successful businessman to date and would be a good, hardnosed operator to have in the business, going forward. Like Previn, Pope also had his own money in the business and this comforted us.

Andrew Allbright was the external accountant with his own private practice. He had been helpful in supplying us with the financial information we needed and agreed that we needed to quickly recruit a full-time finance director.

We liked the other South Africans, Ben Isaacs and David Faber. Isaacs was a long-time friend of Previn and a talented jewellery designer. Quietly spoken and in his early thirties, Isaacs was an equal shareholder with Previn and Pope. David Faber was also an important player, being the key to the retail format, the product offering.

It is fair to say that we had some reservations about how this team would work together if the going ever got rough. But on balance we believed they could deliver the business plan in the five year timescale envisaged. By July 1988 we had completed the documentation and Joe Skrzynski joined SJA's board as AMIL's representative.

The NUMBERS were straightforward enough. In the year to June 1988, SJA achieved sales of approximately $25 million from 25 stores, producing a profit after tax of $980 000. Our first fund, AMIT No. 1, acquired a 10 per cent interest for $1.5 million, valuing the company at $15 million. The gross profit margin on sales ran at a healthy 50 per cent level.

The initial period of operations was encouraging. The existing SJA stores continued their strong performance and the new store rollouts were basically on schedule. By mid 1989 the chain had grown to 62 stores and revenues were $62.5 million for that year. Management had achieved this impressive expansion not only by growth in the number of stores but also by increasing sales per store.

At this point Previn came to his board with a proposal to acquire the Prouds jewellery store business. This business was a long-established industry leader with 104 stores and revenues of $116 million. Previn believed the company would be sold at a knockdown price since its holding company, the real estate empire, Hookers, was headed for bankruptcy. Prouds would be 'on the block'. Previn was highly motivated, not only because he saw Prouds as a desirable acquisition opportunity but because he was most concerned that it should not fall into the hands of someone who knew what to do with it. In other words, he argued that the acquisition was an important defensive move.

For as long as Prouds was run by a real estate owner, Previn did not view it as a threat to SJA. Run by a savvy jewellery merchant, it would be dangerous competition, he reasoned. Previn talked excitedly about the opportunities for economies of scale in management and marketing and especially in purchasing. A combined SJA and Prouds would be the largest jewellery business in Australia, straddling demographics other than just the SJA niche of young females. Once consolidated, the Prouds and SJA chains would represent an attractive public float. By 1992 consolidated sales were projected to reach $300 million, producing earnings before interest and tax (EBIT) of $35 million. An IPO (initial public offering) at that time would provide an excellent exit opportunity. We decided to back management's acquisition plan.

The lenders to the Hooker empire did appoint a liquidator and the Hooker chairman subsequently went to the 'slammer' for various offences. Wardleys was appointed by the liquidator to sell the jewellery business—in a process which ultimately saw SJA emerge with the winning bid of approximately $50 million. This required us to arrange a further equity syndicate provision of $10 million, which we led with an incremental AMIT investment of $3.5 million. Senior debt of $40 million and mezzanine debt of $20 million completed the funding package to provide the necessary working capital. Upon the merger of SJA and Prouds, AMIT's shareholding increased to 18 per cent.

As I look back on this experience, it is clear that from the day the Prouds acquisition was completed the game was over for SJA and for our investment. What went wrong?

Fundamentally, the acquisition was ill-conceived. SJA was a jewellery discounter to a young female market. Prouds was an old established name selling 'upmarket' giftware and jewellery to an older and more conservative customer mix. Quite different business cultures existed in these companies. Attempts at rationalising or merging product ranges were misguided, resulting in the cannibalisation of each other's sales, confusing customers and employees alike. The purported economies of scale proved illusory. The advertising budgets needed to be totally independent to ensure that the two brands survived and prospered. There were no savings there. Prouds had been a steadily declining business; its main stores were shabby and in need of significant capital expenditure for refits. This cash requirement diverted SJA and sank the original SJA store rollout plan.

The original attractive core proposition had been replaced by a fundamentally unsound one. An overstretched management team was very quickly out of its depth. The struggle to deliver rationalisation and economies ensued for several years; sadly, this struggle diminished the effectiveness of both organisations rather than creating an integrated new one with hybrid vigour.

I recall an experience five years earlier when I was CEO of

Barlow Marine, a yacht fittings manufacturer. I was contemplating the merger of a profit-making division of Barlow with what was then the unprofitable Windsurfer Australia company. At Barlow, we had established a sailboard importing subsidiary which had proven to be a very profitable business at the expense of the Australian manufacturer of windsurfers. I thought that the combination of the businesses could make good sense and so I raised the concept with Barlow's principal supplier of sailboards, Will Fischer of the Dutch Ten Cate company. Will was quite negative about my plan and told me of a Dutch expression which translated into: 'If you mix a bucket of clear water with another bucket of muddy water you usually finish up with a bigger bucket of muddy water.'

We knew how to import and market sailboards, but we had no experience in making them. Will was right and we did not proceed with the merger; the Windsurfer company subsequently proceeded into liquidation.

In retrospect, when SJA and Prouds came together they were destined to become one big 'muddy bucket'.

After a debilitating and drawn-out downhill slide, the merged company eventually went into voluntary administration, with the appointment of Ferrier Hodgson. Ferrier Hodgson did a competent job settling with creditors and procuring buyers for the businesses. Basically, Angus & Coote picked up the SJA business and Patons from New Zealand acquired the old Prouds assets.

Of our total investment of $6 million, we eventually received back $2.2 million, proving among other things that not all that glisters is gold.

Lesson one The first lesson from our misadventure is a very old one: *In acquisitions, one plus one sometimes equal less than two.* Critically examine the assumptions about economies of scale and, in particular, carefully inspect the impact of an acquisition on the core proposition that underpins the acquirer.

We had been naïve in backing the management team's merger plan. We assisted in raising the necessary acquisition finance, including approximately $20 million in expensive subordinated debt. This sort of leverage can work extremely well when acquisitions produce results where 1+1 > 2; the same debt leverage is a nightmare when the arithmetic comes out at well under 2, as in the SJA/Prouds union.

Lesson two This important lesson emerged during our extended exit process.

The enlarged business continued to deteriorate in terms of bottom line performance. The acquisition had been heavily leveraged with senior and subordinated debt totalling $60 million. The interest service covenants were breached and the lenders were on the brink of taking over control.

Long before this point, we had realised that we needed to replace the management team and/or sell the business. Sadly, our shareholder agreement did not permit us to do either of these things. This was one of the earliest shareholder agreements in the first AMIT fund; the form of such agreements has since evolved considerably.

So, *always have an exit timetable agreed with the company's owners before you invest*. In the event that the timetable is not achieved, ensure that the shareholder agreement provides a process for the sale of the company.

Absence of such provisions in our SJA documents resulted in unnecessary procrastination and further erosion of shareholder value. We squandered the opportunity to sell the businesses as separate going concerns.

As usual, hindsight is a great instructor. Had we stuck with the original core proposition and organically grown SJA, would the investment have proved successful? Probably yes.

some deals that went wonderfully right

Austal Ships Limited

Early in 1993, in my privileged role as non-executive chairman of the Australian Trade Commission (Austrade), I had the pleasurable task of leading a trade mission to China. Actually, the then Minister for Trade, John Kerin, was really the boss man and his presence meant that wherever we travelled our entourage received the full treatment.

Our start in Hong Kong proved somewhat humbling. The entire trade mission of about 20 business executives, plus the minister, were caught between floors in a lift at the Hong Kong wharf, the lift having decided that further movement was out of the question. Its security phone didn't function and, since it was only 7.30 in the morning, there was no one yet on duty who could hear our best Cantonese calls for help.

The minister, an immense bear of a man at 193 centimetres, commanded that since we were all reasonably large people we should synchronise a jump off the lift floor. This, he explained, would briefly release approximately two tonnes of Western weight from this Eastern floor, to be followed by a reapplied two tonnes as we synchronously returned.

We all thought this was a breakthrough idea, but in practice it proved to be yet another ministerial initiative without results.

Happily, but 45 minutes later, our shouts and tapping led to a rescue and the mission began.

We boarded a high speed ferry bound for Foshan, the nearest port to Ghangzou. This proved to be a fascinating entry into mainland China—travelling up the ever narrowing and busy Pearl River.

So what has all this got to do with Austal Ships and venture capital? Well, I was standing in the stern of the ferry gawking at the huge wash our craft was sending over both sides of the river bank, the water cascading through the houses. Pointing to this embarrassing and blatant abuse, I turned to the fellow standing next to me and said, 'Hell, I'm glad we're not flying an Australian flag on this vessel.'

He replied, 'Oh, I don't know. I built this boat and it's the twenty-fifth one I've sold to China.'

Such was my introduction to John Rothwell, the founder and chairman of Austal Ships. Austal was then emerging as a key player in the fast-ferry business and, along with Bob Clifford's company INCAT, is now a world leader in this exciting and high growth segment of the transportation industry.

When we arrived at Foshan, we attended a ceremony at the Bundy Tube Mill's plant where Minister Kerin formally opened this new installation. Lunch was attended by a variety of Chinese dignitaries including the Mayor of Foshan and related luminaries. All of these gentlemen insisted on sharing a toast, a *campai*, with the minister. One by one during lunch they would come up to the minister and fill his glass with the clear, strong liquid, swallow theirs in a single gulp and invite (insist) the minister to do likewise. To the Chinese delegation's amusement and awe, John Kerin obliged with nine such gulps!

Later during the lunch, I watched him scribbling an important note which he handed across the table. It read: 'Legend travelled through the land, Kerin of the nine campai.'

Rothwell told me of his ambition to extend his shipyard facilities in Fremantle to enable his company to develop a new product, an 80 metre ferry to carry vehicles. Until this time the company had been building 40 metre passenger ferries like the house-drowning one we'd been on coming up the Pearl River.

The CORE PROPOSITION for an expanding Austal was this: fast ferries propelled by jet engines were changing the paradigm of water transportation. As they could travel at speeds greater than 40 knots, these vessels offered cheaper and better solutions than building long bridges or tunnels and were competitive with aircraft over distances less than 200 kilometres. And if the largest vehicle-carrying vessels could be developed, additional commercial demand would be generated. This industry was where aviation was in the 1930s and the prospects were truly exciting.

But why Australian? Why not? The construction was aluminium, lighter than steel, and Australia had the welding and fabrication skills. In hull design, our marine architects were already at the cutting edge. The jets and the materials were at world parity prices wherever the yards were located and, since labour was only around 20 per cent of total costs, Austal could expect to continue to be world competitive.

Furthermore, waterfront land was a key ingredient. The Western Australian Government showed considerable foresight many years ago in designating Jervoise Bay, just south of Fremantle, as a shipbuilding precinct. There is now a cluster of companies with outstanding launching facilities and immediately available waterways for sea-trials prior to delivery. I have visited many shipyards around the world and I don't believe there is any other natural facility in the world that competes with this.

Almost always when I have attended a board meeting in

Austal's handsome head office perched right on the waterfront of Jervoise Bay, dolphins swim by as if to check the minutes of the meeting. I have always taken their presence as a sign of good fortune. And, so far, fortune has indeed shone on this deserving company.

Now, the KEY PEOPLE we would be backing in the proposed venture.

John Rothwell (born in Holland as Rotteveel) migrated to Australia with his family in the early fifties. As a young lad he mucked around in boats and built furniture for pocket money. Later on he tried his hand building a small sailboat and then graduated to fishing boats. With a couple of colleagues he started a small aluminium fishing boat business and sold that to a larger company, part of the soon to be infamous Christopher Skase group.

John did not last long working for others and left to start Austal Ships Pty Ltd in 1987. Curiously, this was the same year that I incorporated Australian Mezzanine Investments with my 50/50 partner, Joe Skrzynski. While 1987 is notorious for the spectacular stock market crash, I think the stars were somehow well aligned for those of us forming new businesses that year.

The Austal founding shareholders were the same team that had worked together previously. In addition to John there were two hands-on aluminium welding and fabrication guys, Gary Heys and Kevin Stanley, plus a brilliant young naval architect, Chris Norman. A few years later they were joined by the fifth key player, a very quiet, very modest and very savvy financial accountant, Michael Atkinson.

Heys and Stanley had no formal qualifications, but were graduates from that famous 'hard knocks' school with boat building skills learned on the job with Rothwell. Heys came to work in jeans and ponytail and on a Harley Davidson. Stanley was the more conservative quiet-achiever type, but both were likable, competent young men who loved building and launching boats . . . on time.

Chris Norman had recently graduated top of his class in naval architecture from the University of New South Wales. Young, clean cut, with great people skills, Norman had been recruited by Rothwell to help Austal find faster hull designs and to head up a sales and marketing function within the company. Selling a $15 million passenger ferry, or a $50 million vehicle ferry, calls for more than just a telephone call or an e-commerce transaction. It is a long and complex process, given the high technology involved in the jet engines and the instrumentation, and the fact that safety and insurance regulations vary from one country to the next. The finance structuring, with performance bonding and progress payment drawdowns, further complicate an already difficult sale process.

Michael Atkinson, the finance director, had arrived in Perth from Zimbabwe and had only recently joined Austal. He was the main source of financial information for Andrew and me; we found him to be polite and open, tending to understate rather than overstate.

This was the team we would be backing with $15 million in expansion capital. Could this team build the larger facilities, produce and sell a new product (the vehicle ferries) and recruit and manage a workforce four times larger? And could they do all this inside five years, with sufficient profitability to justify and organise an initial public offering (IPO) so that we, the financial backers, would have a way out for our investors? Well, art and science might provide some clues.

From the time I first met Rothwell on the back of that ferry on the Pearl River he impressed me with his drive, his confidence and his passion for what he was doing. He was focused—he is still focused! He wants to build a billion dollar shipbuilding business that is not just one of the best, but is absolutely *the* best, in the world. He was consistent in his representations about the company to me and my colleague, Andrew Savage, and handled all discussions and negotiations with the utmost integrity.

Each of the executive team was impressive in his own right and they all unquestionably accepted JR as their leader. So, there was depth, commitment, loyalty, ambition and, of course, they all had their own money in the business too. Our judgement was that this was a special team: they certainly have not disappointed us. Although we did have a short-term scare which I will come to shortly.

I should mention that Rothwell did not have to accept our offer of financial support. He had other venture capital investors to choose among and other offers on the table. He chose us because he wanted more than just the money: he wanted professional and fresh input at board level, a personal sounding board for himself on issues like salary levels and incentive schemes, strategic planning and so on; and he expected networking assistance with government and clients.

I believe we have worked hard to deliver our side of the bargain, but you will need to ask Rothwell if you want an objective view!

Now, let's look at the NUMBERS.

Austal mandated us to raise $15 million in equity capital to facilitate their expansion plans. For this we were offered a 20 per cent interest in the company, valuing the company at $75 million.

As is so often the case, the venture capitalist and the founders/entrepreneurs had a difference of opinion about this starting valuation. Our negotiations on this issue were strident, but never heated. We settled on a formula which was largely driven by future results rather than by past achievements. We have learnt that this approach to valuation can avoid unnecessary disputation about present values; future performance is obviously the key to the outcomes for all participants.

We settled on 10 per cent dividend yielding convertible preference shares, convertible into a maximum of 30 per cent and down to a minimum of 20 per cent of the company's ordinary equity, based on future profit performance.

We decided to be the lead investor, with a $7.5 million investment by our AMIT No. 2 fund in a syndicate we managed. We introduced Prudential Asia out of Hong Kong with $6.5 million and Foundation Capital from Perth with $1 million to complete a strong syndicate of financial investors.

Prudential Asia was an experienced venture capitalist in the region, with a network we believed would assist Austal's sales efforts. Prudential's managing director, Douglas Fergusson, was well known to us and agreed to join the Austal board. He brought loads of energy and multiple networks with him, probably flying more kilometres each month of his life than most jets do. Foundation Capital had recently been established by Ian Murchison as a Perth-based venture capital firm and we were keen to see them succeed, not only because Western Australia needed a local source of venture capital but also because we liked Murchison and his colleagues and believed they would assist Austal locally and keep an ear to the ground for us. This they did.

As events transpired, our shareholding adjustment formula did assist us in securing a fair return for the risks we took. The first year of our investment was a tumultuous one. It was a baptism of fire for my younger colleague, Andrew Savage, who had worked so hard on the project and had championed it with me.

It was a year in which the shipyard moved to newly completed premises and in which the first of the new product, the vehicle ferry, was to be delivered. The employees more than doubled in number, the design office worked around the clock and, in short, the organisation was overstretched.

I must say that I enjoyed the year immensely. The new ferry, larger than a Boeing 747, was called 'The Supercat' and was to be delivered to the big cross-channel operator in Britain, SeaContainers Limited.

Andrew rechristened the vessel 'The Slug' when, in sea-trials, it failed to achieve the minimum contract speed of 38 knots. SeaContainers refused to take delivery and rescinded their contract. We were now the proud owners of a $35 million vehicle ferry sitting at the wharf in Fremantle! Welcome to the world of venture capital.

But Rothwell and his team never lost faith in themselves. They were determined that the engine problems would be fixed, that a redesign of the underwater foil section at the stern of the vessel would enhance performance, and that an alternative buyer would promptly be found. It was a galvanising experience for all of us, and when the problems were solved and the vessel was successfully sold at a better margin than we would have realised with SeaContainers, I knew we had a winning team for the long haul. The hackneyed phrase, 'When the going gets tough, the tough get going', was an apt description of Austal during the early period of our investment.

The key financial figures are shown in Table 1.

Table 1

	Pre-investment year, 1994	*IPO prospectus year, 1999 (forecast)*	*Year ending 1999 (actual)*
	($'000)	*($'000)*	*($'000)*
Sales	87 665	195 681	212 088
EBITDA	9 208	36 234	43 091
Net profit after tax	6 046	21 703	39 832
Employees	500	1 000	1 600

The financial outcomes for our investment are shown in Table 2.

Table 2

	($m)
Investment, 1994	(7.5)
Dividends received	3.5
Sale of 50% shareholding, 1998	17.2
Residual shareholding at market, 1999	15.8
Net profit	**29.0**

Expressed in terms of an internal rate of return, this investment has produced better than 40 per cent. (The internal rate of return is approximately equivalent to the compound annual yield achieved on the cash outlay over the life of the investment.)

An important element in these financial returns was the successful initial public offering (IPO) of Austal in October 1998. For years I had been encouraging John Rothwell and his colleagues to think about and plan for an IPO. John had been reluctant. He saw himself as a hands-on operations guy and did not want to be distracted and frustrated by public participation in his company. Hard to argue with that—unless you want to access capital for expansion, or provide some liquidity for existing investors, or create the opportunity to make acquisitions using your own company's negotiable shares. John slowly came around to appreciating these benefits and ultimately embraced the IPO wholeheartedly.

Austal listed its shares at $1 each in October 1998; one year later the shares were tracking at $2—a high speed performance. Particularly pleasing in this IPO process were the profits enjoyed by the several hundred members of Austal's workforce who acquired stock.

Lesson one *If you back high quality people you are more likely to get a high quality outcome*. This sounds trite, I know. Perhaps a less banal way of putting it is this: You must assess your entrepreneur and his team in terms of how you think they will cope with unexpected setbacks. You want them to hang in there, not just because their money and reputation are on the line, but because they actually love the challenge. And Rothwell and his team, I'm glad to say, thrive on it.

One of the real joys for me in this venture capital business has been the experience of successfully working through good and bad times with entrepreneurs. Without the bad times, you don't know how good 'good' is; the lessons learned through the bad days are often more valuable than those of the good days.

Lesson two This lies in the analysis of the core proposition. We were right in the analysis that suggested that this fast-ferry sector should enjoy a high growth decade or so and we were right about Austal's competitive position. *Pick a fast-moving stream and hop in where the current is with you*.

Lesson three A third lesson relates to *structuring the deal with a future-performance-based shareholding formula*. This clearly helped us to cope with the risks, with the huge uncertainties involved in plant relocation, new product introduction and pioneer marketing. The willingness of the entrepreneurs to share this risk rather than insist on a fixed valuation upfront made it possible for us to step up. They now have a smaller share of a much larger and more successful pie. Rothwell's equity is worth about $80 million at 1999 market prices. Who says you can't make money out of manufacturing in Australia?

Education and Training Australia Pty Ltd

This deal came to me from an old and close friend, the lawyer Peter Kemp. PK, as he has always been known among his large and diverse group of friends, built up a very successful corporate legal practice over many years in Sydney. Kemp Strang is a second tier firm with a solid reputation for liquidation work, conveyancing and general corporate practice.

PK and I once owned a turf farm on the Colo River, about an hour and a half from Sydney. Nestled in the calm and beautiful Colo Valley, this property was the source of much fun during the seventies and eighties. It turned out to be more successful at growing losses than growing turf, for shortly after our purchase of the farm the valley suffered a one-in-100 years flood. Exacerbating this hard luck story was PK's indefatigable practice of ploughing. He loved to plough. He would roam over the fields with the tractor, in the process ploughing over most of our underground sprinkler outlets and ultimately destroying much of the tractor and its ancillary equipment. Libel laws restrain me from offering further anecdotes about my farming partnership with PK; let me just say that I would not hesitate to send you along to his firm for legal advice, but I would send you elsewhere for investment advice.

So you will understand my apprehension when PK rang one day saying that he had a 'great deal' for me to look at.

PK had a client called Barry Tilley, a powerfully built man with a do-or-die, fear-nothing style in the way he conducted himself. Both Barry and his drop-dead attractive wife were very entertaining company. One quickly came to the view that Barry would always lead a 'colourful' life.

Tilley and another colleague had invested some 'punt money' in a business called Careers Business Colleges Pty Ltd (Careers). Careers had been started in 1986 by a Canadian entrepreneur I will codename Hank.

Careers was like a private TAFE—TAFE being the government-funded Tertiary and Further Education system. It was a privately owned enterprise offering certificate and diploma courses in a range of vocational studies such as Tourism, Hospitality, Computers and Word Processing, Commerce and Marketing. It also provided English-language training for overseas students.

The CORE PROPOSITION was this: while the TAFE system would continue to provide vocational studies on a heavily subsidised basis—for example a diploma course costing $5000 at Careers might cost only $500 at TAFE—the demand for such services would outstrip the government's willingness and ability to fund.

Furthermore, the relatively bureaucratic and inflexible TAFE system would never suit many candidates: mostly young people who preferred to be treated like a customer rather than as a student number, and who expected to get a job as soon as they graduated.

Careers had been successful, in each of the three years prior to our investment invitation, in placing more than 90 per cent of their students into jobs.

Another part of the core proposition related to the market for foreign students. It was projected that more and more overseas students, particularly from Asia, would travel to Australia for English studies and subsequently for a vocational qualification. The playing field was level in this market in the sense that, unlike the TAFE domestic students market, Australian taxpayers were not subsidising the fees of the offshore students and so Careers was free to compete.

I needed little convincing with respect to this prospect of rapidly expanding foreign student business. One of the early successes for the Australian Trade Commission (Austrade) when it was created in 1985 was its push to open up Australia to foreign students. Prior to that time, apart from a small number of postgraduate students, there were virtually no visas available for overseas students. The Austrade team completed a persuasive analysis which demonstrated the size of business being lost at the time to Britain, Canada and the United States. Australia had the credibility, reputation and teaching resources; it also had the geographic advantage of proximity to the Asian market, where English-language training was the highest-growth product in the region. What was needed was the political will to relax our temporary-immigration laws and to persuade the Australian community that the foreign students would not displace Australians from education and training opportunities.

The first minister during my term as chairman of Austrade was John Dawkins, who had become Minister for Education. Dawkins was a prime mover in Cabinet in getting the necessary changes through and, as a result, Australia now has an industry in foreign student education worth $1 billion and more per annum.

So, although there was significant private and government competition, we liked Careers' core proposition. The company had established a profitable business with strong cash flow, had an enviable record in achieving job outcomes for its student customers, and was in a fast-flowing river.

And what about Careers' KEY PEOPLE? We used to refer to them as the Three Musketeers, all likable, highly entrepreneurial, swashbuckling characters. I have already described Barry Tilley. His investor partner was a very experienced retired lawyer, Tom Cahill. Tom had been a schoolboy boxing champion, was still very fit at 65, and was now a skiing enthusiast. I liked him from the start and, although he was always a non-executive director, he turned out to be an important player—as I will explain later.

The key man, however, was the founder, the Canadian-born entrepreneur—Hank. In his late forties, Hank was a handsome and hard-driving operator, the quintessential salesman with that motivational can-do North American style. Hank could make his sales people feel as if they had filled their quotas even before they left the weekly sales meetings. He believed, so they believed.

Hank's attractive brunette wife featured in the television commercials promoting the company's services, and she was actively and effectively engaged in sales and sales training. They were a formidable team.

The Three Musketeers had done pretty well building the business in five years to a $10 million sales enterprise. Some of my investment committee colleagues, Joe Skrzynski and Professor Jeremy Davis in particular, had doubts about the

Musketeers' ability to develop a large corporation when organisational challenges of structure, management information systems and so on could prove beyond Hank's skills and experience. Joe said he had a 'feeling in his *kischkas*' about all of this.

Earlier in our twelve year partnership, Joe and I had agreed that we would not invest in anything that left either of us feeling uncomfortable. The deal had to feel right for *both* of us in our *kischkas*—a Yiddish reference to somewhere in your guts. In the end Joe's discomfort dissipated, but in the meantime it influenced our ultimate structuring of the transaction.

Nick Greiner, AC, former Premier of New South Wales, accepted our invitation to join the Board as chairman. Nick and I were classmates from Harvard Business School days and I knew of his interest in and knowledge of the education sector. His skills and contacts turned out to be all-important when this investment hit choppy waters.

But first the NUMBERS. We were invited to subscribe $3 million, providing $1 million to the existing owners and $2 million for new capital to expand the business. After much 'argy bargy' with the Three Musketeers, and in part to settle down Joe's *kischkas*, we subscribed only $2 million for 25 per cent of the company's capital. Three years later we subscribed for a further $0.8 million and advanced an additional $5.4 million to facilitate an acquisition. In 1997 we sold our $2.8 million equity stake to a larger competitor for $8 million. A summary of these flows is shown in Table 3.

Table 3

	($m)
Original equity, 1992	(2.0)
Additional equity, 1995	(0.8)
Loan, 1995	(5.4)
Dividends and interest received	2.6
Loan repayments	5.4
Sale proceeds	8.0
Net surplus	**7.8**

This surplus produced an attractive IRR (internal rate of return) over our six year investment period of 29 per cent.

But, oh, what a roller-coaster ride this deal turned out to be! For the first year or two after we made our investment all seemed to be on track. Student numbers grew, good profits were earned and cash surpluses expanded. Note that this is a business with no inventory and no receivables. Students pay a portion of fees upfront and the balance during the course of their studies. This makes the business largely self-funding. Of course, investment in the infrastructure of lecture rooms, computer networks, curricula development and advertising was significant; hence the need for our involvement.

But then the numbers began to slide. The company had been supporting a subsidiary in Indonesia which did two things. It acted as a sales office to secure Indonesian students (primarily Chinese Indonesians) to study in Australia and it also conducted English courses in its small college located in a suburb of Jakarta. This Indonesian operation was a cash hole, but because Indonesian student numbers in Careers' Sydney campus had expanded to more than 500, the company had been reluctant to close down the loss-making Jakarta office.

I asked my colleague, the experienced AMIL executive director Su-Ming Wong, to visit the Jakarta operations and to make immediate recommendations. Su-Ming was disappointed to find a mess: the financial records were non-existent; the Australian general manager had resigned, leaving the business in the hands of untrained local employees; the furniture had been seized by police on the grounds that certain business licences had not been properly applied and paid for. These licence payments were in fact a form of 'protection money' that had previously been administered by the expatriate general manager but which the local employees refused to go along with. One of the local employees was hospitalised following one of these 'police' visits. All in all, Su-Ming concluded that we had to either significantly expand the operation in terms of numbers and quality of both management and teaching staff, and relocate the campus to the Chinese district, or otherwise immediately close the present operations down. We chose the latter course of action and made alternative arrangements for attracting Indonesian students to Australia.

The next problem was more serious and systemic. Following the Tienanmen Square riots and killings in June 1989, Prime

Minister Bob Hawke granted amnesty to some 25 000 Chinese students who had been studying in Australia and had 'gone missing'. Political and community pressure concerning the maladministration of foreign students in Australia intensified. There were numerous examples where the student visa process was being roundly abused. Asian students might pay their enrolment fees to a private college, obtain entry to Australia, attend classes for maybe two or three weeks and then go AWOL. There was evidence that some private college operators were quite active in this trade; after all, this was attractive, high margin business for dodgy operators—fees upfront and no students to bother the teachers!

Against this background, we were advised at a board meeting called to review declining numbers that several of our key sales agents were redirecting business to colleges where the rules and protocols were more 'lenient' than ours. We became concerned that this competitive pressure might lead to a slackening of our own protocols. (Records had to be rigorously maintained and the immigration authorities immediately advised if a student fell below an 85 per cent attendance rate. Strict legal obligations applied, with serious consequences for the company directors if breaches were allowed.)

Therefore we commissioned an independent firm of accountants, Mann Judd, to review our practices and protocols and to make any necessary recommendations to ensure that Careers complied with the relevant regulations.

Shortly thereafter, Hank received a call from a television company, saying that they were going to run a story on the 'foreign student visa scams' and wanted to do an interview on the Careers campus. The team was from *A Current Affair*, a leading prime-time current affairs program.

Hank declined the offer to appear on the show and called a meeting to discuss the development. It became clear that the program people had the chairman of Careers, former premier Nick Greiner, in their sights for maximum impact and controversy. To a lesser extent they also had me lined up, as the immediate past chairman of Austrade, the organisation that was one of the architects of the foreign students program.

We had two big concerns. The first was the immediate

commercial one. It was September and we were coming up to the peak selling season in the domestic market, when school leavers and their parents would be making the decision on what college to select. Then, in the December/January period, came the peak enrolment period for offshore students. Negative press could not come at a worse time and might even prove fatal.

The second concern was whether there might be some truth in the allegations and whether Careers could be implicated in the story about manipulation or abuse of the visa laws.

We asked Mann Judd, the accounting firm, to complete their report as a matter of urgency. Nick Greiner agreed to have an initial 'off the record' discussion with the television journalist in order to get a fair understanding of what was being alleged. Unfortunately, however, the program was run that night, prior to any discussion with Greiner or the company. It was a terrible story, full of innuendo and unsubstantiated allegations, and replete with pictures of the directors and so on. Welcome once more to the world of venture capital!

We became very angry. The accountant's systems review came to us the next day and, while we were relieved that they'd found no evidence of regulatory abuse, we were shaken by their comments about the many *opportunities* for abuse and the insufficient checks and balances in our current data collection and reporting systems.

In spite of our formal protests to the television channel and requests for right of reply, the program was aired again and trailers were run heralding a follow-up report for the following week. The damage to our business was becoming substantial. We briefed legal counsel, applied for an injunction to prevent any further programs being aired and threatened to sue the television company for damages to our own company and to Nick Greiner's personal reputation. Finally we had the television company's attention.

Nick Greiner was unflappable and resolute throughout this drama-packed three weeks. He and I held discussions with the television executives and a settlement was rapidly agreed. No more programs, and a formal apology by the channel went to air.

This put out the fire, but as we were to learn over the ensuing six months, we were left with fire-damaged goods.

Domestic enrolments collapsed to less than 50 per cent of the previous year's numbers, although we were able to hold the foreign student numbers at about 80 per cent. The impact on cash flow was immediate.

But there was more bad news. Following the television show, we received a note from a student alleging that falsification of attendance and academic records had occurred in one of the college's diploma courses. The board confronted Hank with the letter and its evidence and simultaneously instructed the accountants, Mann Judd, to investigate the matter. To cut a long story short, one of the head teachers was guilty on all counts and furthermore had, in our view, obtained Hank's tacit co-operation in that endeavour. While only ten students' records had been manipulated in this fashion, out of perhaps as many as 3000 in that year, nonetheless it had happened. If that sort of cancer appears in an organisation, you have to cut it out, there and then. If that means the top has to go, then all the more important that the surgery be swift and decisive.

It is said that the life of a venture capitalist is incomplete until he has had the task of replacing a portfolio company CEO. This experience was an awkward one. Hank was the founder and he was still the single largest shareholder, with 40 per cent of the company. His leadership had been found wanting but he would argue that the matter was grey, not black and white—that he had not personally pocketed anything, that he was just meeting the competition, that it would never happen again, and so on.

However, our unequivocal view was that he had placed us all at risk, jeopardising the entire company in the process, and that we were not prepared to live with a 'grey' code of ethics. Furthermore, the company was now going to need a further cash injection from the shareholders or otherwise collapse. It came down to a shootout at high noon—either Hank had to buy us out or we had to buy him out. In the event, Tom Cahill and Australian Mezzanine Investments together purchased Hank's shareholding and obtained his immediate resignation as CEO.

Tom Cahill was another exemplar of the old saying 'When the going gets tough, the tough get going'. Tom still believed in the business and its core proposition. He was as angry as we were about the way it had been mismanaged. He put in some more money with us when it was needed. He and I effectively ran the business for the next three months, co-signing every cheque, selecting new advertising formats, and generally keeping the show on the road until such time as a new CEO could be found.

The task of finding a CEO fell to me. As luck would have it, I stumbled on the right person at just the right time in his career. By extraordinary circumstance, the new CEO, Arvid Petersen, was also a Canadian. I had met Arvid in the Young Presidents Organization in Sydney. He had just completed a five year contract as CEO of Pepsi Cola in Australia and was now looking for a fresh opportunity where he could make an investment in a smaller business that he could build up. Why not Careers?

Arvid negotiated a good entry price, investing several hundred thousand dollars of his own money to buy an equity stake of 20 per cent. He hopped into the fray as CEO and began the tough job of rebuilding reputation and share. The Careers name, for so long an asset, had become a liability. Such is the power of a prime-time television story!

We needed a bold move to re-establish the business in its rightful place as a leader in the private college sector. I had known Lorraine Martin for some years, having arranged for her appointment to the Board of Austrade. She had successfully built a Queensland private college business which enjoyed a market leadership position and a well-deserved reputation. Lorraine had previously raised with me her desire to sell her interests one day and perhaps pursue other activities. After discussions spanning a year and a half, we completed the acquisition of Lorraine's business, which effectively doubled the size of the company and provided it with campuses in Cairns and Brisbane together with a high quality network of offshore agents.

Arvid set about the challenge of capturing the best from both organisations and driving for economies of scale. This involved a transitional change of trading name to Martin College, which today has campuses in Cairns, Brisbane, Gold Coast, Sydney, Parramatta and Melbourne.

To facilitate this acquisition and rebuilding strategy, we had by December 1995 increased our investment by $6 million.

Midway through 1997 we received an approach from British Study Group, the education arm of London Daily Mail Co, to buy the business. The CEO of British Study Group, Andrew Colin, was a bright, articulate, no-nonsense young man who got on famously with Arvid and wanted him to continue on as the CEO of an enlarged group encompassing some of BSG's Asian activities as well.

As the venture capital providers, we had concluded that, given the hiccup in earnings and growth of the enterprise during the adverse television phase, an exit via public flotation was no longer an option. The attraction of a trade sale was therefore compelling and we moved promptly to close a fair transaction with British Study Group. This sale realised $8.2 million for our shareholding, against a cost base of $2.7 million.

Lesson one *If the time comes when you need to fire the CEO, don't procrastinate*. When the problem became clear, the one thing we did right was move quickly and efficiently, so limiting the opportunity for ongoing damage to the enterprise. We found a new CEO with integrity and drive, one who was given the benefit of the doubt by the media, the sales agents and the employees. This gave us a breathing space to enable the company to deliver on its original core proposition, a proposition that was always valid and ultimately delivered a very profitable outcome.

Lesson two This point relates to the composition of the Board. *It is almost always best for the new money to have the right to appoint the chairperson*. From the outset, we insisted that Hank step down from the chair in favour of our appointee. When things become difficult, when fundamental disagreements among the shareholders emerge, a strong chairperson has a very important role. Nick Greiner played that role with skill and courage—we hope he will continue to be involved with other parts of our portfolio, perhaps with less controversy and tumult.

Lesson three *Before you invest, always be sure that you have at least two realistic and alternative exit tracks*. Had we relied only on an IPO exit, we would have been frustrated by the media damage inflicted on the company. That experience would have rendered an IPO, at best, deferred and discounted and, at worst, impossible. A trade exit, by way of a sale to an existing competitor or a new entrant, was always in prospect for this business—that is, if the core proposition was valid somebody would want our market share and our established infrastructure and distribution setup. As it happened, selling the business was not difficult.

Lesson four A further lesson based on this venture (and many others) is: *The opportunity for a venture capitalist to truly add value to a portfolio company is directly proportional to how badly that company is doing*. The company that is travelling well, with a strong management team in place and the tide of events going with it, presents relatively limited opportunity (or need) for significant value to be added by the venture capitalist. If it works, don't fix it. If it doesn't work, move quickly to see what you can salvage and rebuild. The art here is, on the one hand, not to give up without a thorough assessment of your salvage chances, and on the other hand not to go on flogging a dead horse.

In the present case, we were able to make a realistic assessment of what could be done to save and rebuild the business and we were able to add value significantly. We replaced the CEO, we identified and executed a smart acquisition opportunity, we arranged the necessary incremental funding and we negotiated a very successful sale price on exit.

And we sold just prior to the Asian meltdown of October 1997, so I should add that Lady Luck was on our side too. The venture capitalist who tells you that luck has never played a key part in his or her successful deals is either a liar or about to have a real bad day.

Cuppa Cup Vineyards Pty Ltd

For more than a decade we had searched for a venture capital opportunity in the exciting Australian wine industry—always without success. Typical reasons were the capital intensiveness of the business, the land development costs, the time to first commercial-volume vintage, and the investment required in brand building. These factors usually combined to produce negative cash flows and low investment returns.

Frustration after frustration! We love to drink wine, we love to pretend we know something about it—you know, the *terroir*, the late picking, the length on the palate and all that—and we certainly believed that this industry represented the best agribusiness opportunity for Australia since the Merino wool innovation of over 150 years ago.

During my years as chairman of Austrade, the organisation worked with the wine industry and developed an export business plan predicting that Australian wine export sales would reach $1 billion per annum by 2000. This was sceptically received by many at the time, but the prediction has proved pretty accurate. Wine exports in fact topped $1 billion in 1999, a remarkable achievement by the industry.

In 1994 Paul Riley and I met with the past chairman of the Australian Wine & Brandy Board, Robert Hesketh. Robert had been a partner with two other wine men, James Herrick and Mark Swann. These three pioneered the exporting of Australian wine to California, eventually with some success. They sold their export distribution business to a larger Australian group and embarked on their own grape production enterprise in South Australia.

They purchased 200 hectares in the area of Bordertown adjacent to the now world famous Coonawarra district. Enjoying similar *terra rosa* over limestone, and Murray River irrigation, the vines prospered and successful harvests of cabernet, shiraz and merlot were achieved. The group signed a take-or-pay style of contract with Penfolds, providing a steady cash flow which was intended to fund the realisation of a far more ambitious and innovative vision.

Encouraged by James Herrick's prior experience in the French wine business, the group developed a bold plan based on three premises:

1 Wine country in the Languedoc region of France was very

cheap when compared with prices in the famous *appellations* such as Bordeaux, Champagne, Burgundy and Chablis. This was in spite of its high quality soils and generally very favourable conditions for wine growing. The region suffered from a *vin ordinaire* reputation, with a veritable sea of red grape production. The team believed that this relatively cheap land could produce high quality grapes and wines.

2 Australian wine growing skills and wine making techniques could be applied to the Languedoc district, involving broad acre farming (with high trellises and frost controls) where previously only small (four hectare) sub-economic plots existed; and using stainless steel tanks in production, where old and cracked concrete vats were the norm.

3 Varietal wines could be successfully promoted, still with the 'Made in France' cachet, where *appellation* geography had until now been the prevailing product description. In particular, Herrick was convinced that a chardonnay could be marketed. Believe it or not, there were no French chardonnays available on the market. Indeed, of approximately one million hectares planted to wine worldwide, by 1991 fewer than 100 000 hectares had been planted to chardonnay!

   The group believed that a French wine marketed as a chardonnay varietal would be very popular in Britain. Australian varietals had already proved successful in this large market; why not a 'Made in France' chardonnay produced by Australians?

These three premises formed the CORE PROPOSITION for their French enterprise.

Five years and many millions of dollars after embarking on the pursuit of this vision, the group needed more money—and so my story really begins here. Robert Hesketh explained the good news and the bad news to Paul Riley and me; we had to work out whether the core proposition had ever made sense and whether it could still make sense.

But first—what about the KEY PEOPLE?

Hesketh, a likable and knowledgable identity in the Australian wine industry, gave us a straightforward pitch with negligible gilding of the lily. His steady and usually phlegmatic behaviour (at least by comparison with many others in the industry with whom we had dealt over the years) was to prove important. The industry has a healthy share of prima donnas, winemakers who regard customers as somewhere between ignorant and irrelevant, accountants as oozing carbuncles on all human progress, and financiers as leeches to be spoken to only when all else fails.

Hesketh's colleagues, Herrick and Swann, occasionally stray (or is it swagger) into this prima donna profile. At such times, Hesketh is fairly artful in running around with buckets of water to throw over everybody until temperatures can be reduced to talking levels.

Actually, Herrick beat up on me only a few times; what's amazing is that, every time he did, I realised afterwards that he was more right than wrong. James Herrick is a handsome man in his mid-thirties with an attractive personality and a good degree of style and joie de vivre. It is his name on the bottle, his heart and soul in the product inside and his anatomy on the line. James *is* the company, in the sense that he runs the French vineyards and winery and is the key executive to whom all the distributors, wine writers and creditors wish to speak.

I first met James at his winery at the La Motte vineyard just outside Narbonne in the Languedoc. Someone had to go to the south of France to do the due diligence work and, as is often the case, this onerous task fell to me. A flight from Paris to Toulouse, followed by an easy two and a half hour drive on the motorway, takes you past the walled mediaeval town of Carcassonne, alongside the Canal du Midi and into Narbonne. Along the way, you go through wine country whose vines have been providing the peasantry with jobs and hangovers for over 1000 years.

After my long trip from Sydney, James received me politely if a little perfunctorily. After all, he had a lot of wine to make and sell; besides, the essence of his business plan was so bloody brilliant that one would have to wonder why any venture capitalist wouldn't just do the deal over the phone. James didn't actually say these words, but I saw them in the body language.

It was that evening which provided me the best due diligence, the most relevant insights into Herrick and his colleagues. We were all invited to share a cassoulet and a wine tasting at the country house where James and his family live, on the La Boulandiere estate owned by the company. The cassoulet prepared by James's attractive American wife, Simone, was delicious. The wines had been selected and masked by our host. Dinner guests were the venture capitalist and potential financier, namely moi, Robert Hesketh, Mark Swann, and a man who turned out to be very important for the ultimate financial success of the company, Trevor Mallett, the finance director.

The wine tasting proved great fun if a little embarrassing for me. I was able to tell the difference between a red and a white, and I did pick the one Australian bottle from all the rest, which were French. I was amazed that Hesketh and Swann could actually identify vintage years, grape varietals, winemakers and the *appellation contrôlée* in each instance.

But more important than these skills was the camaraderie, the strength of the personal relationships, the respect for and enjoyment of each other, and the obvious fondness and high regard with which Herrick was held by all of them. I reckoned that, if these relationships had survived and strengthened through the difficult financial period they had experienced in recent years, this was indeed a good sign.

I should add, lest you think that sipping wines was the extent of my due diligence, that I was thoroughly impressed by the quality of the engineering of the vineyards and the winery. Both were beyond my expectations—the company clearly had outstanding assets.

On a subsequent visit to the winery, this time as a director and one year after our initial investment, I was accompanied by Ken Allen. Ken was an external director appointed by us and someone who we believed would assist the process towards corporate governance and ultimately public flotation. During this important board meeting at the La Motte winery, Herrick accused Ken and me of not having read the board papers, of unreasonable delay and obfuscation in approving a red wine expansion project, and generally of being unhelpful. Ken has had a successful career in investment banking and, while he had in fact read the board papers, it is fair to say he kept his focus on the big picture issues, not on all the details. A big man of disarming charm, he handled the contretemps admirably: his suggested adjournment for lunch proved to be deftly timed.

Two years later, when we were planning the initial public offering, it was Ken's idea that we should invite the wily investor and experienced businessman, Grahame Mapp, to be the company's independent chairman at the time of the IPO. Ken had been a key player for County NatWest when it successfully floated the Petaluma wine company and was well equipped to assist our IPO efforts. Thankfully, Grahame accepted the invitation, adding experience, discipline and credibility to the float process. He insisted on improved corporate governance, but in a manner that kept the entrepreneurial essence of the company intact.

(A quick aside about the IPO prospectus. During the extensive and painfully slow due diligence process involved with the offering document, the solicitors required objective verification of 165 different statements made by the directors. One of these related to the opening statement in the offering memorandum: 'The chairman is pleased to bring this opportunity . . .' But was the chairman actually pleased? This we had to verify! Happily, Grahame Mapp *was* pleased; and he continued to be pleased as the share price of Cuppa Cup settled sensibly above the offering price.)

Trevor Mallett is the other key figure. Trevor is really Herrick's right hand man; a softly spoken, somewhat shy person, Trevor knows the numbers inside out and speaks up firmly and unhesitatingly when he needs to. With the company's borrowings in Australian dollars and French francs, with domiciles in France, the United Kingdom, the Netherlands and Australia, with sales revenues in sterling, French francs and Australian dollars, with principal assets in Australia and France, Trevor has had his work cut out hedging the exchange risks and managing the various accounting consolidations. For a small company, it has big complexity and the group has been fortunate to have a man with Trevor's experience and talents.

Which brings us to the NUMBERS.

The costs, delays and frustrations in the establishment of the French operations had more than offset the previous three years' $5 million profits from the Australian vineyards. Indeed, shareholders funds of about $2 million had been eaten up and the company was technically in default of various loan documents with its Australian and French bankers.

At the time of Hesketh's invitation to us, the company had borrowings of approximately $18 million, assets of around the same and annual revenues of approximately $4 million. The company urgently needed working capital in the order of $5 million to fund its growth plans and to settle down some sceptical bank lenders.

After long and difficult negotiations with the Herrick/Hesketh team, we agreed on a $1 million redeemable convertible preference share arrangement entitling us to a 50 per cent shareholding, accompanied by a subordinated loan of $1.5 million and a guarantee to support a UK overdraft facility of $2 million. All of this was conditional upon the company first securing an agreement to a 'haircut' (debt forgiveness) of approximately $1.5 million from one or more of the principal lenders.

Three years later, at the time of its successful IPO in July 1998, the company was capitalised at $27 million and our shareholding was worth approximately $9 million. We sold back half our shareholding in a company buy-back arrangement concurrent with the IPO.

During my weeks on board the ketch in Turkey in June 1999, the company received a takeover offer from the Southcorp group. My mobile phone took a thrashing; after the usual amount of argy-bargy, the board decided to recommend the Southcorp bid at $1.35 per share, subject to no higher bid being received.

Our IRR on the investment now exceeds 50 per cent—a very successful vintage indeed!

Now, let's return to the core proposition.

When James Herrick arrived in Narbonne in the late 1980s and announced that he was looking to buy some properties, or *domaines*, the local people were somewhat bemused. But he found three separate *domaines*, in aggregate some 200 hectares, with appropriate soil and water rights. These were *domaines* with long established vines, all of which Herrick proceeded to remove. He also fumigated the soil. At this point, the locals' mood of bemusement shifted to one more of agitation. Then, when Herrick finally had 200 hectares of broad acre chardonnay vines in full leaf, complete with fencing and trellises, things turned rather nasty. Guns were fired at and through the vineyards; sheds and equipment were graffitied; and threats were made against Herrick himself.

This behaviour of the locals mystified Herrick until one day in a Narbonne bar he learned that the annual district *chasse* had been effectively ruined by the Cuppa Cup development. Shooters and their dogs were unable to pass through the property. Herrick rapidly made it known that during the two or three week hunting season the shooters would have free access into and through the vineyards. End of problem.

After some other project delays, the first and second pieces of the core proposition had been delivered: Herrick had demonstrated that this Languedoc land could be bought at an economic price and was indeed capable of supporting a high quality chardonnay varietal.

Herrick then had to prove the third part of his proposition—that a demand for wine from this region could be established in the UK market. Not surprisingly, convincing the key buyers in the specialty chains like Oddbins and Victoria Wines took longer than first thought. The 1993 vintage was small and somewhat experimental; it was really not until the 1994 vintage was available that the buyers became confident of the sustainability and quality of the James Herrick label. The big retailers TESCO and Sainsbury also bought the product as it began to establish a position at the premium price point of £3.99 a bottle.

The fundamental pieces of the core proposition were beginning to work. There was only one problem—the company was now running out of money. Hence the possible opportunity for Australian Mezzanine. Was the project ever really going to work or, once again, was the industry just too competitive for us, too capital intensive? This was the stumbling block that had thwarted our previous attempts to find a venture capital opportunity in the wine industry. The returns were always too far off and too low. But in Cuppa Cup's case we reckoned that most of the hard vineyard and wine development program had been completed, and very professionally so. If the lenders would take a realistic view of their debt and provide some debt forgiveness, the returns could still be there. So we agreed to provide funding for the company, including some for debt retirement, provided that Herrick and his colleagues could first convince one or more of the banks to agree to a 'haircut'. This was eventually negotiated and so the company was provided the wherewithal for a final chance.

The company used our money well. Extension of winery capacity, new product introductions including a shiraz, Cuvée Simone (named after the cassoulet chef), and an investment in promotion were all successful. Case sales grew from 25 000 in 1995 to almost 100 000 in 1998. The core proposition was bold and it was right; our funding assisted the realisation of Herrick's vision and the IPO allowed the development to continue.

So, is there anything to be learned from this intoxicating investment tale?

Lesson one *Patience is still a virtue*. I mean this in two senses. First of all, we waited for many years to find the right opportunity in the wine industry. Those years were not wasted, since we had gathered together some worthwhile industry data and contacts which were useful in gauging the Cuppa Cup project. This patience equipped us to recognise value when it came along and when others did not see it.

The second reward derived from our patience with a talented and at times mercurial chief executive. James was difficult and perhaps precious from time to time. Yet we never doubted his integrity or his commitment; we learned to bite our lips occasionally (I think my colleague Paul's lips are still bleeding), because James actually does hear the other points of view—eventually.

Lesson two *Timing is more important than analysis*. I must say I'm not sure my close friend and partner, Joe Skrzynski, necessarily agrees with this point. Joe has a powerful intellect and, in my experience, unmatched powers of analysis across a broad range of industries and technologies. And when he's firing, cerebral sparks fly. I remember one day when we were flying to New York together. On the runway at Mascot before takeoff he was giving me a headache with an animated description of a technical software business. The flight attendant was at the same time asking passengers to turn off their mobile phones, laptops and other such equipment which interfere with aircraft instrumentation. Finally, I had to say to Joe, 'For God's sake, stop thinking until after takeoff!'

Joe's cerebral energy notwithstanding, I believe timing is all-important. And it happened that when we were encouraging/requiring Cuppa Cup to achieve a debt forgiveness, one of the lenders was closing its European office and seeking to close off all receivables. This fortuitous circumstance played to our advantage.

A second piece of fortunate timing was the strength of the equities market and the voracious appetite for new issues during the first half of 1998. This also played well to our hand for, although Cuppa Cup was of small capitalisation (approximately $30 million), the IPO was well supported. And the takeover offer from Southcorp at $1.35 per sfare represented a 50 per cent premium over the issue price of 90 cents just twelve months after the IPO.

Lesson three *A well-structured shareholders agreement never needs to come out of the files.* One of the key points in our agreement with the founders was the timetable for realisation of the investment. A timetable and a commitment for realisation are important for all shareholders but especially for the minority non-executive shareholding of the venture capitalist. Otherwise, the venture capitalist is exposed to the whims and passions of the majority holders.

Our bargain with Herrick and his colleagues was unambiguous in this regard: Here is our money with which to finish the job you have so impressively started, but let's have it back within five years or the price goes up. Needless to say, the legal talent (in this case Andrew Stevenson at Corrs Chambers Westgarth) expanded this understanding into innumerable pages of complex clauses!

Stevenson said to me several years ago, no doubt trying to justify his fees, 'The better your transaction documents, the less likely it is that you will ever need to pull them out of your desk.' This homily has proved to be correct over the years. (It proves painfully true in the reverse also.)

The Cuppa Cup founders were true to their word. Although James referred to our shareholders agreement as the 'Australian Mezzanine Sword of Damocles', it did act as a sensible discipline for everyone in the value-creation obligations we shared.

Lesson four *Personal 'money up' focuses the mind.* Nothing you haven't heard (or perhaps felt) many times before, but well worth repeating. The executives and founders of the company had a very high percentage of their individual net worth in this deal; in at least one case, that percentage was greater than 100 per cent.

Success in this venture, particularly in turning it from the brink of insolvency to a profitable public company, required risk taking, good luck and loads of hard work. Whether at harvest time (when Herrick literally works around the clock), or at wine promotions, or at investor meetings, the fact that the founders have their own money in the venture has maintained their focus, their commitment and their energy level. And the same has happened in our case, I might add.

Datacraft Limited

Datacraft has been a great success story for us and for the venture capital industry in Australia. We invested $3.5 million and received back more than $30 million over our seven year engagement with the company.

Established in 1974, Datacraft was already a publicly listed company when it was first brought to our attention by the well-known and highly respected stockbroker, Gilles Kryger. Gilles' company, Ord Minnett, had been broker to the initial public offering of Datacraft shares in 1985. In 1989, the company was in need of funds for expansion, but an attempted rights issue had failed to achieve support. The shareholders had become disenchanted with the company's variable performance, and small technology companies had about as much appeal to the institutional investors as a Rumentek beef steak has to a vegetarian.

Datacraft had ridden an early wave of demand for modems, 'black boxes' enabling computers to speak to each other remotely by transferring large volumes of data down telephone wires. These black boxes were in high demand and Datacraft was successfully manufacturing and selling them throughout Australia. When we were invited to consider supporting the company's rights issue in 1989, the business was roughly $60 million per annum in sales and making a modest profit.

The problem was that modems were rapidly becoming commodities, with declining margins and prospects. Still, something caught my partner Joe Skrzynski's eye about this particular company.

Since starting the first AMIT fund in 1988, we had identified the IT and telecoms sector as a high priority. We believed it was a sector which could offer higher than normal returns for venture investors. This belief was founded partly on the predicted explosive growth for the sector as a whole in Australia over the decade of the nineties. It was also based on our own direct experiences and contacts confirming the significant research and development base in Telecom, CSIRO, Defence and elsewhere. There would have to be opportunities for smaller companies to commercialise some of this work and to obtain profitable niche positions in the coming market explosion.

Joe was convinced that Datacraft could be one such company. Not because of what it presently made and sold, but because of what it could do building on existing expertise and credibility.

The CORE PROPOSITION was as follows. The requirement in the corporate world for local area networks (LANS) and wide area networks (WANS) was an immediate and escalating one. There was a proliferation of equipment suppliers, of computers, of telephones, of routers, of modems and so on. What would be needed in Australia and in Asia was a credible company to be a systems integrator to design and implement these communications networks. Customers were bewildered by the choices, alternatives and complexities—a credible and independent operator (one independent from any one hardware supplier) could charge handsomely if it could deliver systems integration that really worked. Furthermore, such an operator might also derive very attractive maintenance fees to keep these systems live. Such a maintenance business might prove particularly attractive in the disparate economies of Asia if a multinational company could call a Datacraft help-desk and know that the same screwdriver would be used in Bangkok or Kaoshung or Guangzhou.

This was an exciting proposition which, if successful, would see modems represent only 10 per cent of Datacraft's business within five years compared with 90 per cent in 1989. Joe believed the founder and CEO, George Kepper, was on the right track. What was important and became our opportunity was that nobody else seemed to understand Kepper's concept or believe in it. As a consequence, Datacraft's 20 cents issue price had sagged to 14 cents and the rights issue at 20 cents had no chance.

We were able to negotiate a funding alternative to the proposed rights issue whereby we advanced $3.5 million to the company by way of a 14 per cent interest bearing note, convertible into shares at our option at 20 cents each within five years.

There were several KEY PEOPLE in the Datacraft team—in research, manufacturing, finance and sales. The two key players, however, were George Kepper and the boss of the Hong Kong–based Asian subsidiary, Des Althorpe.

George Kepper is a charming, phlegmatic, careful and clever man. His only non-business activity that worried me (apart from his lack of interest in golf) was his passion for flying. He owned his own plane and I was alarmed to learn that occasionally he would fly himself from Melbourne to Sydney for board meetings. Our core proposition was at 12 000 feet in a small owner-operated plane! Fortunately, George brought the same meticulous planning and operating style to his flying as he did to his business.

Prior to starting Datacraft in 1974, George's career included five years in Europe as an electronics design and project manager at Ericssons and then a period as general manager of a division of Fairchild Semiconductor back in Australia.

George was always the majority shareholder right up until the day the company was sold in 1998. After full conversion of our convertible note, he would still own in excess of 51 per cent of the company.

Des Althorpe, the other key player, was an Englishman and a chartered electrical engineer. Des had worked with British Telecom and then Telematics International in Europe. Kepper recruited him in 1987 to be the managing director of a wholly owned Datacraft subsidiary, Datacraft Asia. I believe this was the single best action Kepper took as chief executive, as Althorpe proved to be a real winner. Of medium build, Althorpe was a dynamo, ambitious and hardworking and a tireless motivator of others. He told Joe and me of his plans to establish Datacraft offices right through Asia, from the top of China all the way down through Indonesia. He believed that the data collection and transfer requirements of Asia were immeasurably large and that Datacraft Asia would have to grow at 40 per cent per annum compound just to keep up.

By the time we were completing our due diligence, Des had established profitable offices in Hong Kong, Singapore and Kuala Lumpur. He was well advanced with the planning for Beijing, Bangkok and Taipei. It was difficult not to believe that here was a man in the right place at the right time.

In short, we were impressed by the core proposition and by the two men vital to the delivery of that proposition. But what about the NUMBERS? In 1988, the year immediately prior to our investment, the Datacraft performance was as shown in Table 4.

Table 4

1988	*Sales ($m)*	*Profits ($m)*
Australia	38.4	3.3
Asia/NZ	22.3	3.4
Unallocated expenses	–	(2.5)
Group	**60.7**	**4.2**

With approximately 77 million shares on issue, the company had a market capitalisation of just $10 million. We agreed to advance $3.5 million by way of a 14 per cent interest-bearing note, convertible into 17.5 million shares or roughly 20 per cent of the company. Kepper remained the largest shareholder with a controlling 70 per cent diluting to 55 per cent upon conversion of the AMIT notes.

In the year immediately prior to the company's acceptance of a takeover bid in 1998, the figures were as shown in Table 5.

Table 5

	Sales ($m)	*Profits ($m)*
Australia	66.2	3.2
Asia/NZ	183.9	16.2
Other	20.5	(3.7)
Group	**270.6**	**15.7**

With approximately 110 million shares then on issue, the company was capitalised at $330 million at the offer price of $3 per share. Kepper's holding was worth about $160 million. Consistent with our philosophy of realising profits on the way up, we had achieved the outcome set out in Table 6 for our investment.

Table 6

	($m)
Initial outlay	(3.5)
Dividends and interest received	2.4
Share sales, 1993–97	7.6
Sale at takeover, 1998	18.4
Net profit	**24.9**

This provided us with a very satisfactory IRR of approximately 40 per cent over the seven year life of our investment.

The outstanding value creation occurred in Asia. The Australian manufacturing activities had continued to show poor margins and the systems integration business began to suffer from an invasion of international participants. Kepper's core proposition had been right, but he no longer had it to himself in Australia.

As a consequence, the long-suffering Datacraft shareholders in Australia again lost patience and the stock price sagged for lack of interest. This sagging price was a concern since the company needed more funds to fuel the continuing high growth of its Asian business. The trick was how to uncouple the two companies and access the arbitrage that existed between the valuations enjoyed by Asian IT companies and those suffered by small Australian IT companies.

Joe hit on the idea of a partial float of the company's Asian subsidiary on an Asian stock exchange. This would enable us to access earnings multiples closer to 20 times on the Hong Kong and Singapore stock markets, compared with the single digit multiples then afforded to companies such as Datacraft in Australia.

Althorpe was red hot for this idea. He could see that unless he could uncouple from the Australian parent he would never be able to realise the growth potential of the Asian business, nor could he achieve personal wealth for himself and his management team. Des enthusiastically supported Joe's plan and together they eventually convinced George of the wisdom in the idea.

George was understandably nervous about having *two* stock exchange listings, about issues of control, transfer pricing and other responsibilities complicated by the existence of two separate groups of shareholders. We assisted in the design of appropriate protocols and governance procedures for all these matters and enlisted George's now enthusiastic support.

The offshore listing proved to be a milestone in the value creation process for all Datacraft shareholders. We selected a venture capital group well known to us in Hong Kong and Singapore who could help in the process of the Asian float. This was the Transpac group headed by Christopher Leong. Transpac subscribed for a private placement of approximately 10 per cent of the capital of Datacraft Asia and subsequently introduced the Development Bank of Singapore to be the sponsor for a public listing twelve months later on the Singapore stock exchange.

In March 1995 Datacraft became the first US$-denominated listing on the Singapore exchange. The IPO was priced at US39 cents a share, valuing the Asian subsidiary at US$71 million. Des Althorpe and his team always hit their prospectus forecasts and continued to grow the company at 40 per cent compound. Offices were opened in mainland China, South Korea, Japan, India, Thailand, Taiwan and Indonesia. Datacraft Asia thus became the only systems integrator that could offer a multinational company an Asia-wide maintenance and quality control service for its data networks.

By early 1997, less than three years from the Singapore listing date, Datacraft Asia's shares had moved past the US$2.00 mark; that is, more than five times the listing price. The Asian subsidiary, then 60 per cent owned by the parent, was valued at approximately $500 million on the Singapore market, while the Australian parent was valued at only $133 million on the Australian stock exchange. One of the markets had to be wrong and we held firm in our view that eventually Australian investors would recognise this arbitrage opportunity. Arbitrage refers to a divergence in price which can occur for the same product on different markets at the same time. Such apparent imperfection in the markets may create opportunity for investors to make an 'arbitrage profit'.

In order to create more liquidity in the Australian share register, I had begun to sell several million of our shares into the market during 1994 at prices between 50 cents and $1.10. This practice was also consistent with our philosophy of bagging some profits on the way up.

While this partial selldown created more institutional interest in the Datacraft Australia shares, the large arbitrage position between Asia and Australia remained unresolved. The riddle remained: how were we and the rest of the Australian shareholders ever going to be able to capture any benefit from this arbitrage?

The Datacraft board advised shareholders that it was actively analysing various scenarios: reverse takeovers, sale of the Asian company with return of capital, and other recapitalisation schemes. In the end, a takeover offer was received from the large South African group, Dimension Data. Dimension Data bid $3.00 a share for 100 per cent of the company and were successful in obtaining the board's positive recommendation to shareholders. This recommendation was forthcoming, inter alia, because the bid was at a price that once and for all solved the arbitrage riddle.

AMIT sold its shareholding on market at the bid price, realising $18.4 million for its residual shareholding.

This investment was a success on many counts: in terms of jobs created, exports generated, millionaires created in the management teams in Australia and Asia, and returns to the investors.

The lessons learned from all of this were many; the two most important for me were as follows.

Lesson one This point has been made already but, in spite of its obviousness, deserves emphasis. *High quality people get you high quality outcomes.*

Kepper never lost faith in himself or in his company even during serious setbacks and even when the public investors deserted the stock. In 1996 the company had missed its budgets badly, the Australian company racked up abnormal losses of $6.5 million and the company's bankers had become concerned with the group's lack of cash flow. This was a time when Kepper personally provided extra collateral to keep the bankers at bay and to provide the company the time it needed to prove itself.

Althorpe, of course, has proved to be a quite exceptional chief executive. He moved seamlessly from being a private subsidiary CEO to being a public corporation CEO. Leading by example, he delivered 40 per cent compound growth in sales and profits and ultimately created outstanding value for both Asian and Australian shareholders.

Lesson two The second lesson was *the importance of thinking beyond just the Australian markets when planning the investment exit.* This point is discussed at greater length in the next chapter. In the case of Datacraft, I'm refering to the listing of the Asian subsidiary in Singapore, not the ultimate sale of the holding company. The Asian float captured an earnings multiple twice that available at the time in the Australian market. This facilitated an efficiently priced expansion of the Asian company enabling it, inter alia, to purchase more equipment and services from its Australian parent.

I mention this aspect because of the concern, often expressed in the Canberra bureaucracy and elsewhere, about Australian companies moving offshore. Much of this discussion is unbalanced, in my view, if the alternative would be stunted growth and a failure to access global markets. If such an alternative is the Australian solution then badge me un-Australian.

LookSmart Inc.

LookSmart is the salvaged wreck of a Readers Digest division. It began as a farsighted internet initiative by Readers Digest and sadly lost its way and all of its champions within that group. Then in 1995 along came a bright and energetic McKinsey IT consultant, Evan Thornley, and his wife Tracey Ellery, who offered to take it off Readers Digest's hands in return for taking on the responsibility of ongoing funding.

In the same year that the Thornleys made their purchase, Sequoia Capital, a leading Sandhill Road venture firm in California's Silicon Valley, completed a $1 million investment for 25 per cent of another internet company that had no business plan, no revenues, and nothing that it could sell. This company was a search engine business called Yahoo! and by early 1999 Sequoia's $1 million was worth $8 *billion*, probably the most spectacular venture return of all time. Sequoia was obviously not put off by strange names, as it had earlier financed a little company called Apple.

Thornley's vision, which became the CORE PROPOSITION for the company, was simple. Although influenced by Yahoo!, the proposition was different. Thornley believed there was plenty of room for a search engine that could get people to where they needed to be on the internet in a quicker and friendlier way than the other available search engines could. Furthermore, Thornley felt that LookSmart could deliver higher quality information by the prior editing of websites and other databanks. Given enough editors, he believed, LookSmart's buildup of information would ultimately constitute a proprietary franchise of considerable value to users and hence advertisers. He would build an internet media company with a proprietary database.

Okay, but how was LookSmart so different from, say,

Yahoo! or Lycos or Alta Vista, all of which had such a head start? Why would they allow LookSmart into the game?

The core proposition involved the following ambitions:

- The company's category-driven (as compared with word-driven) search was aimed at maximising e-commerce usage by also capturing user data such as prior purchase behaviour. LookSmart would continue to build on Readers Digest's direct marketing skills. LookSmart's proprietary dynamic server architecture was built around the need to capture, analyse and respond in real time to user behaviour data to optimise e-commerce revenue performance. This same user data would also assist the company's ability to attract quality advertisers.

  Thornley's advertising model was to some extent borrowed from Yahoo! In an interview with David Kaplan (*The Silicon Boys*, Allen & Unwin, Sydney, 1999), Sequoia's Mike Moritz reflected on his decision to invest in Yahoo! Moritz said, 'Maybe too simply, I just felt you're in your car listening to radio for free or you're at home watching CBS for free. So why will the Internet be any different? The trick, strategically, was to get an audience and retain the audience and at some point the advertisers would come.' And come they did.
- LookSmart was unique among navigation services in adopting a 'syndicated and distributed' traffic strategy. This distinguished it from the big brand competitors like Yahoo! and would enable the company to quickly reach profitability.
- LookSmart had invested for two years in a team of 25 editors to provide it with a proprietary database targeted at consumers over 30 years of age. By rapidly expanding its investment in the editing process, LookSmart intended to establish the largest proprietary database of edited websites in the world. This database could be licensed to the likes of Microsoft and Excite, so providing a secure revenue stream additional to the less certain advertising revenue.

LookSmart's pursuit of these ambitions would provide it with a defensible and profitable position in a dramatically expanding internet market. If the proposition was sound,

LookSmart could occupy this space alongside much larger players such as Yahoo! and Excite because its product was sufficiently differentiated.

The KEY PEOPLE who would make all this happen had mightily impressed one of my co-directors in AMIL, Paul Riley. Paul was the first believer and had to work overtime convincing the rest of us that LookSmart could really be a winner in such a competitive business. Like most successes, there is no shortage of champions who emerge after the event. I can nonetheless claim that I did encourage Paul to bring the project forward to the investment committee. Paul was the one who really stuck his neck out, as much because of the calibre of the key people as his belief in the core proposition.

Paul's quiet speaking style is sometimes mistaken for uncertainty of view and resolve. In fact, he has a steely 'dog with a bone' approach to many things, one of which was the LookSmart proposal.

He was very impressed with Evan Thornley, as were Joe Skrzynski and I. Thornley had spent four years with McKinsey in that firm's telecommunications, consumer goods and energy practices. He became a leader in the global online advertising practice group and led internet training programs on strategy and corporate finance. Evan had formed LookSmart in 1995 and had been its leader ever since. The big question for us was: could he make the step from successful consultant to effective chief executive officer?

Being a McKinsey alumnus myself, I was naturally predisposed to liking Thornley. Unlike Thornley, who had earned his McKinsey stripes the hard way, I can only lay claim to a good fun 'summer job' at McKinsey between years at the Harvard Business School. I had been recruited into the firm by two of the School's illustrious Australian graduates, Roderick Carnegie and Dr Timothy Pascoe. Rod and Tim were both brightly shining comets in the McKinsey galaxy at that time and I was excited by the opportunity to learn more about the firm. In 1969 I worked the three month holiday break in the New York office. The main assignment was for a new McKinsey client, Mr Kerkorian, then the owner of MGM. He was trying to work out how to improve the probability of producing profitable movies. It turned out that after the smash hit of Dr Zhivago, MGM's next 50 movies were all unprofitable. All 50 had been over budget on cost and under budget on revenues. So Kerkorian called in McKinsey.

We prepared an elaborate matrix of all the studio's movies for the previous 30 years. Love stories against revolutionary backgrounds were the top scoring category—over westerns, comedies, spy dramas and so on. Kerkorian already knew this and so, while this piece of work was intellectually rigorous, it did not by itself take the client very far.

Thornley had more success with his clients at McKinsey and deserved his star reputation in the firm.

Evan's wife, Tracey Ellery, was the co-founder of LookSmart and had overseen the development of what was widely regarded as the best subject index on the Web. With previous experience in computer retailing, market research and publications development, Tracey was obviously a key player from the start.

Thornley had recruited Brian Cowley as VP Sales & Distribution. Cowley had headed advertising sales for the Netscape website and brought directly relevant experience to the LookSmart challenge.

The chief operating officer was Martin Hosking, who was also a McKinsey alumni. Like Evan and Tracey, Martin was from Melbourne where he had completed his undergraduate and MBA studies.

This was the team we would be backing. Thornley was the boss and he was the face to the external market. Articulate and intellectually vigorous, he preached the LookSmart story to any and every audience. My first experience of Evan's oratory powers was at a meeting in our George Street office in The Rocks, Sydney.

Paul Riley had badgered me to come to this meeting. 'At least say hello and have a brief meeting with Thornley, who is in Sydney today and on his way back to San Francisco,' Paul had insisted. Well, what was intended to be a fifteen minute hello and goodbye became a fascinating hour and a half presentation about LookSmart, its problems and its prospects. Thornley rarely drew breath and made a lasting impression on all of us. He told us that he had at least six weeks' working capital because the company's cash burn was 'now only $400 000 a month'. Talk about life on the edge!

Which brings us to the NUMBERS.

When we were in discussion with the company during the last quarter of 1997, the actual daily page views generated by the LookSmart engine had begun to demonstrate rapid acceleration. From fewer than 250 000 daily page views in September, LookSmart enjoyed over one million in December 1997. These were projected to grow to eight million by December 1998 if the company delivered on its core proposition.

Of great interest to me were two other important operating numbers. The advertising revenue per visitor was already a high 13 cents compared with a competitor average of 4 cents. And because of its leveraged distribution strategy, the company had achieved these revenue results with a cost base equal to one-third that of Lycos and one-fifth that of most others.

Monthly losses of approximately $500 000 in December 1997 were projected to fall progressively towards breakeven mid-way through calendar 1998, as advertising revenues responded to the positive direction in page view usage. The company's balance sheet showed only six weeks' working capital remaining; shareholders funds had fallen from just under $7 million to approximately $2 million.

The company wanted to raise US$4 million and was offering a 25–40 per cent shareholding for this amount—valuing the company in the range US$10 million to US$16 million. When I think back to the difficulty I had in justifying this valuation to myself, it seems amazing that only twenty months later, in August 1999, Goldman Sachs priced the IPO on NASDAQ at US$12 per share—a capitalisation of almost US$1.3 billion. At the end of its debut trading on Friday, 20 August 1999, LookSmart was valued at US$1.7 billion or A$2.5 billion! This proved to be the highest IPO capitalisation of a technology company in the history of Australia. By October 1999 the company's share price had doubled again and the market capitalisation stood at an astounding A$5 billion.

Available benchmarks for valuations at the time of our initial investment were internet company trade sales and IPOs, which were priced at multiples ranging from 10 times revenue to 45 times revenue. Annualising December 1997 monthly revenue of $250 000 valued the company at between $2.5 million and $12 million. On projected December 1998 revenue the company could be worth between $20 million and $100 million. If the investment market's interest in internet companies was sustained, we could see a prospect for making ten times our money if LookSmart delivered on its core proposition.

So we agreed with Paul that there ought to be a place somewhere in our portfolio for an investment in LookSmart. We decided it was best suited to our recently formed innovation fund, AMWIN, which was a partnership fund with the Walden International Investment Group of San Francisco and the Australian Government. We decided to invest US$1.5 million via AMWIN, provided that our Walden colleagues were happy and that not less than another US$1.5 million could be found from another investor.

There was little time left as LookSmart was scheduled to run out of cash within a matter of weeks. We therefore pushed the Walden Group to complete their due diligence rapidly. Walden's CEO is a nuclear physicist and a trusted friend of ours by the name of Lip-Bu Tan. Like AMIL's executive director, Su-Ming Wong, Lip-Bu is a Malay-born Chinese and has an outstanding record of success in the early-stage venturing business in the United States, Asia and Israel. One of his colleagues just happened to be a key player in organising the IPO of Yahoo!. This was Steve Eskenazi who, at the time of the Yahoo! IPO, was working for Morgan Stanley.

Steve was well placed to understand the valuation templates and to gauge market appetite. While he liked the LookSmart people and its story, it is fair to say that Steve was less than enthusiastic. He was concerned that LookSmart might be too late and too small to make the impact that it envisaged for itself. Nonetheless, Lip-Bu decided to back his new Australian partner's judgement and so the AMWIN participation was approved. Securing the balance of the monies proved to be more difficult.

We had hoped and expected that our friendly venture capital competitors, Allen & Buckeridge, would be our co-investor.

Roger Allen and Roger Buckeridge became disenchanted with one aspect of the terms sheet and rejected the final position drawn in the sand by Evan Thornley and LookSmart's lawyers.

Notwithstanding this disappointment, we decided to go it alone and we remained optimistic that LookSmart's discussion with the big US cable group, Cox Cable, might soon lead to a co-investment by this strategic player. But just how serious were Cox likely to be and would they come on board before the cash ran out? As circumstance would have it, the CEO of Cox, Jimmy Robbins, was a long-time friend of mine, having been my room-mate in our Harvard Business School days. Jimmy is a 193 cm, no-nonsense guy who has been in cable all his business life. 'Ferro,' he boomed over the phone, 'our guys really like this LookSmart thing and we'll be there despite Ozemezz beating us to it!'

Indeed, Cox ultimately provided the extra money to LookSmart and has proved to be a strong and supportive shareholder ever since.

As well, we'd always considered Cox the likely trade buyer in the event that the stock markets for internet companies did not hold up long enough for us to succeed with a LookSmart IPO on NASDAQ.

And what happened with this LookSmart deal? My colleague, Paul Riley, is still smiling from ear to ear, if that is any clue.

Six months after AMWIN's initial investment of US$1.5 million, we followed up with an AMIT No. 2 investment of another US$2 million. The company aggressively pursued its commitment to a proprietary database, increasing the number of editors from 25 to 65. Accompanied by content and a style that proved especially attractive to female navigators, and a business model offering syndicated links on a co-badging basis, LookSmart was succeeding in consolidating a position in the top twenty websites worldwide.

We were delighted when the company recommitted its navigation service to exclude all pornographic and hate material. It was not only a morally sound position but also one that was important to women and to parents.

Pursuit of the syndicated and distributed traffic strategy was accelerated by acquisitions of companies offering website developers suites of products enhancing sites and traffic flows. BeSeen.com, for example, was a Texas company with products such as Hit Counter (measuring the number of hits on a site), Chat Rooms and Quizlets (allowing mini-polls to be conducted online).

Perhaps the key decision in 1998 was whether to pay US$6 million to Netscape to be designated one of their premier search sites. We worked on this analysis, with Paul Riley supporting Evan in LookSmart's board decision to make what was then a major capital expenditure decision. This move was to result in a rapid increase in traffic to LookSmart.

All of these developments were being successfully undertaken by Thornley and his team during 1998 and captured the very close attention of Microsoft. Towards the end of calendar 1998, Microsoft negotiated an access arrangement whereby it would license LookSmart's proprietary database of URLs (universal resource locators) for a fee of approximately US$80 million over five years. This was a non-exclusive licence and did not lock LookSmart into Microsoft.

This arrangement was consummated in the first quarter of 1999 and it was then clear to all that LookSmart was headed for an IPO.

LookSmart's Board invited formal proposals from Goldman Sachs, Hambrecht & Quist, Morgan Stanley and Robertson Stephens. Once again we at Australian Mezzanine were able to provide valuable input to Evan Thornley in the IPO process. The managing director of Morgan Stanley in Sydney, David Kent, was a long-time acquaintance of ours. He introduced Paul Riley to Rex Golding, then visiting Sydney from the Menlo Park office of Morgan Stanley. Rex liked the LookSmart story and persuaded his colleague in the New York office, Mary Meeker, to meet Thornley. Meeker is regarded as something of an internet guru in investment banking circles and her endorsement was valuable to the IPO underwriting process. Morgan Stanley's interest and enthusiasm stirred similar emotions in others. Ultimately, the mandate was given to Goldman Sachs as lead underwriter, who indicated an IPO valuation of approximately US$1.2–1.5 billion.

While this selection process was going on, we decided to lay off some risk by selling our free warrants in LookSmart for approximately $8 million to the Gresham Media Fund. We did this not out of any concern for the company as such, but rather from our anxiety about the stock market generally and the internet company valuations specifically. Our creed over many years has been 'Never be too greedy'. Expressing this another way, a handsome book profit always takes on an especially welcome flavour when converted to cash. As a result, the numbers at the time of the IPO in August 1999 were as shown in Table 7.

Table 7

	At US$12 IPO value (A$m)	*At US$36 Oct 1999 value (A$m)*
Initial investment	(2.2)	(2.2)
Follow-up investment	(3.2)	(3.2)
Sale of warrants	7.9	7.9
Current shareholding	92.2	276.6
Net profit	**94.7**	**279.1**

A gain of between $95 million and $279 million on an outlay of $5.4 million in a period of less than 24 months is not too shabby! Of course, we won't really know where we stand until the six months post-IPO 'lock up' has passed, as only then, in March 2000, will we be free to trade the shares.

Once again, timing emerges as highly important factor in these outcomes.

When the buttons were pressed by Goldman Sachs for Evan Thornley to commence the LookSmart roadshow in the first week of August 1999, market conditions looked propitious. Some internet stocks had shown a few wobbles, but overall the Dow Jones, the S&P100 and NASDAQ continued their stellar performances of the record 1999 year. Thornley marched off with his presentation kit on a tour that would take in London, Frankfurt, San Francisco, Los Angeles, Phoenix, Chicago, Boston and New York. As each day progressed, so the market grew more volatile and weaker. The issue was due to be priced on Friday, 13 August 1999 in New York, but that turned out to be the 'week from hell' for internet stocks. The first three days of that week witnessed significant falls in the leading internet companies, including AOL, Yahoo! and Amazon. Of 40 scheduled IPOs that week over 30 were withdrawn, including ours. The market then picked up again on Friday and we all held our breath over the weekend. If Monday the 16th was strong, then just maybe the IPO could be reinstated in the week ending 20 August. Well, luck was with us and the demand for LookSmart's offering firmed up rapidly, enabling Goldman Sachs to price the IPO on Thursday and establish a listing on Friday the 20th.

This day turned out to be one of amazing timing for Paul Riley. The critical board meeting of LookSmart directors to authorise the IPO and fix the pricing, attended by representatives of the underwriters, Goldman Sachs, was set for 6.30 a.m. on Friday, Sydney time. This happened to be exactly the time Paul was scheduled to attend the birth of the Rileys' first baby. Paul took the conference call in the hospital while his wife, Irene, was entering the delivery room. He rang me at 6.55 a.m., to report the good news, namely that 'both IPOs were on track'. Goldman Sachs had committed themselves to get the LookSmart IPO completed that day at US$12 per share and Irene was on target for the IPO (Irene & Paul Offspring) of a baby girl, Eden, who one day will understand her well-earned nickname, IPO.

Of course, many others had been eagerly awaiting LookSmart's market debut. Every LookSmart employee had a stake. About six weeks after the IPO I visited Evan Thornley, who showed me around the five buildings that LookSmart then sprawled through in the South of Market area of San Francisco. Once a garment and mixed manufacturing precinct, this area is now a hotbed of internet startups occupying converted warehouses and employing thousands of young people in occupations that did not exist two years ago.

Hundreds of these young graduates sit at their screens researching and editing websites and databases for LookSmart. I was struck by the quiet and professional focus of these people, few of whom even met my gaze as we strolled by. Evan asked me how it could possibly be otherwise when every single person on the LookSmart payroll had stock and/or stock options in the company. 'No better way to make sure people are motivated and focused, and likely to stay with you,' Evan remarked.

When Evan was called off to another meeting, his assistant Teresa wanted to know what I thought of the about-to-break US$35 million LookSmart television campaign. She ran the video featuring the Beatles' song 'Help!' and encouraging family viewers to solve their diverse information needs through LookSmart. 'Help!' was a my-generation hit and the commercial looked perfect to me. But why, I asked, was the song delivered by a female rather than by the Beatles?—a reasonable question given that the company had paid US$3 million for the rights. Teresa reminded me that LookSmart was the first-choice search engine for a majority of female users in the United States and the company intended to entrench this support.

LookSmart is on a bold adventure to establish its brand and accelerate the growth in numbers of users. So far, it is the only Australian company that has established any sort of internet brand position internationally.

Well, there ought to be some worthwhile lessons from such a happy outcome, ones which might lead us to the next LookSmart deal.

Lesson one *The venture capitalist needs to think globally when it comes to exit time.* If you have a business that is global, in terms of its markets and its competitiveness, then you must think of the capital markets in a similarly global context. It is not un-Australian to arrange an Australian company's IPO offshore. At the time of writing, LookSmart has a market capitalisation on NASDAQ of A$5 billion and it has an additional $150 million in the bank as a result of the IPO. It has established new high-water marks in the history of Australian technology companies by these achievements. Such numbers would not have been achievable from the local markets.

There is a fair amount of fuzzy thinking on this issue in Canberra and elsewhere. The Australian fear of losing technology offshore is understandable, given our nation's long history of outstanding inventiveness but poor commercialisation. This issue is further discussed in Part Two of the book.

However, the surest way for us to fritter away the benefits

of Australian innovation would be to deny Australian entrepreneurs access to the deepest and best priced capital markets. Companies that are unable or unwilling to exploit their innovations widely and rapidly are likely to be swamped in the marketplace or by technological obsolescence or both.

Converting intellectual property into bottom line outcomes is more about timing and the dominance of a niche marketplace than it is about patents and lawsuits. The successes of Australian companies like Cochlear, the 'bionic' ear implant business, and ResMed, the sleep apnea treatment business, have obviously been assisted by the original breakthrough research done by Graeme Clark and Colin O'Sullivan respectively. Their science and the patents arising from it formed technology platforms for these great companies. But it was the pioneering marketing work done by Paul Trainor and Michael Hirshorn that established Cochlear's sustained leadership position in the US, Japanese and European markets. And the energetic, even frenetic, marketing accomplished by Dr Peter Farrell is what established ResMed in its leading position in the sleep disorder markets of North America.

While Cochlear successfully arranged its IPO in Australia and enjoys strong investor support, ResMed chose to IPO on NASDAQ where the appetite among investors for this type of company was so much stronger. Farrell still runs ResMed, the Australian production plant has been expanded to cope with bigger export volumes, the number of Australian employees has increased and, importantly, the sustainability of the company's market position has been enhanced.

'Born global' high technology businesses, especially internet ones like LookSmart, are presently well supported by NASDAQ. Realistically, the Australian company should have a significant proportion (probably not less than half) of its revenues derived in US markets and should be prepared to relocate its CEO and head office to the States. This is a prerequisite for the considerable information flow expected by US analysts and for achieving necessary investor interest and support in that market.

It will not always be the IPO markets in North America that offer the best outcome to Australians. Back in 1995, as noted in the previous chapter, we arranged the IPO of the Asian subsidiary of Datacraft Limited. We were forced to look outside Australia as the local market had lost interest in the listed parent company. The US market was not really suitable since Datacraft's US activities were only nominal. Therefore we turned to Hong Kong and Singapore as alternatives.

Often the Australian stock markets will be the *right* IPO solution, as they were for other portfolio companies of ours such as Cuppa Cup Vineyards and Austal Ships. But whether or not this is the case, at all times the venture capitalist must think globally when it comes to exit time.

Lesson two *Don't be greedy!* Unlike entrepreneurs' budgets, things don't always go up. Markets don't always stay in bull cycles and not all surprises are happy ones. In short, to use a current American technical phrase, shit happens.

At AMIL we have always adopted the approach of leaving something on the table for the next investor and of taking some profits on the 'way up'. We have seen many examples over the years where fortunes have been made and lost, where markets have collapsed more quickly than they rose and where extraneous events have devastated values in spite of blameless and dedicated performance by management teams.

When the opportunity recently presented itself for us to sell our free warrants in LookSmart and bag an $8 million cash profit, we took it. This decision retrieved our capital outlays twice over and left us still holding all of our shareholding in the company.

Lesson three Again, *timing is more important than analysis*. As sound as our analysis of the LookSmart opportunity and core proposition was (and I think Paul Riley will reluctantly agree), we never really expected the interest in internet companies to explode in the way it did. When we committed to LookSmart we thought our upside could be ten times our investment, if everything went to plan. As it happened, we should realise more than 50 times our money!

The venture capitalist who does not admit to luck playing a significant part in his successful deals is either a true genius or deluding himself. How many true geniuses do you know?

Of course, we had looked at several internet investment opportunities prior to LookSmart. We had built up a certain level of understanding and confidence before we took the plunge and we have continued to seek out and invest in this area. This experience and sensible analysis will hopefully help us to avoid the internet lemons, but I have no doubt that timing and luck will be a key to finding the next LookSmart.

the twenty most important lessons—so far

What follows is a summary of the twenty major lessons I have learned from the various investment adventures described in this book. On balance, I have probably learned more from the disappointing investments than from the successful ones. Perhaps that mirrors life generally: you learn quickly from your bruises or otherwise get very badly hurt.

The lessons as set out here are not intended to reflect any order of priority.

1 *Leopards don't often change their spots*. The idiosyncrasies of head-strong entrepreneurs invariably become more pronounced

over the years. Success confirms their habits and foibles; failure seems to do likewise. Don't assume that your venture capitalist cheque book or personal charms will fundamentally change any behavioural patterns or 'spots' of the CEO.

2 *High profile shareholders/partners do not by themselves make a deal successful.* Prestigious and credible names on the share register may bring comfort to lenders or suppliers, but they often have their own agendas and their own core business pursuits which, over time, diverge from those of your investee company. This divergence or lack of interest can spell big trouble for the investee company, especially in times when the going gets tough.

3 *A venture capitalist's financial returns are not always inversely proportional to the distance between his office and the investee's head office.* This has been my experience with many of our most profitable investee companies situated far away from our Sydney offices—in Perth, Melbourne and San Francisco. And our worst investees have been as close as a block away in Sydney and as far away as Fiji. I decided to include this lesson in the list because the myth has grown up that venture capitalists only like to invest in companies within 45 minutes driving time.

4 *Beware of solutions looking for problems; the marketplace is more important than the science.* The challenge for early-stage investors in new technologies and processes is to be able to identify the strength and timing of actual commercial demand for the solutions that these new things purport to offer. It can be very expensive to be years ahead of the market.

5 *Have the courage to know when to stop flogging a dead horse.* I use the word 'courage' because it can be all too tempting to chase a failing deal with more bad money. It can be very hard for you to accept the investment for what it is, a failure. On the one hand, the venture capitalist should not give up on an investment merely because of temporary setbacks; but

on the other hand, he or she must learn to judge when enough is enough. Most people can only learn this on the job, not from reading books like this one.

6 *Never let a pathological optimist be the CEO.* The entrepreneur who genuinely deludes himself is ultimately more dangerous than the one who actually knows the truth but sets out to delude you.

7 *High quality people get you high quality outcomes*, especially if they have their own money on the line. Although this sounds trite, it is a recurring key lesson. If a high quality and experienced management team is in place, be prepared to pay full price for the deal. If there's a low quality and inexperienced team, chances are that no price will prove to be cheap.

8 *Critical analysis of the venture's core proposition is what distinguishes a sensible 'risk investment' from a 'punt'.* The time and effort you expend in really getting to grips with the fundamental business proposition, with working out whether the business really does have a sustainable competitive position, will be rewarded over time. You will still have the occasional failure, but generally you will produce excellent results for your investors.

9 Having said that, the good deals don't stay on the table for long in what has become a very competitive venture capital market. Ultimately, *timing is more important than analysis.* It would have been easy for us to develop analysis paralysis and never make an internet investment. But we did plunge in to the rapid and wildly flowing internet river. Here, as elsewhere, timing and luck played a very large part.

10 *Build future performance adjustments into your deal structures.* If you do this, your ultimate equity entitlement in a venture will depend on the venture's future performance, not on its past glories or on its wonderful forecasts.

11 *If the time comes when you need to fire the CEO (or some other key executive) of an investee company, don't procrastinate.* Every time I finally decided that a key executive was not right for the job, I took too long to make the change. Having made the change, I invariably looked back and asked, 'Why didn't we insist on that sooner?'

12 *An independent director usually makes a better chairperson than the entrepreneur CEO.* This lesson has been most pronounced in situations where the enterprise is not performing well. When the respective interests of external shareholders, employee shareholders and lenders diverge, the need for an independent chairperson becomes greatest.

13 *Prior to making an investment, be confident that you have no fewer than two alternative exit tracks.* As a venture capital investor you are usually a minority shareholder in an unlisted company, and without pre-agreed exit timetables and plans you can easily find yourself 'locked in' with nowhere to go.

14 *The opportunity for the venture capitalist to really add value is directly proportional to how poorly the investee company is performing.* Even when things are going to plan, the venture capitalist can usually still add value in the boardroom and elsewhere. A strong and organised management team can leverage off fresh ideas and inputs; but in the main such a team will achieve the business plan anyway. It is really when things go wrong that the venture capitalist has a big opportunity to help and to salvage value.

15 *Patience is still a virtue.* Here I'm actually referring essentially to the pre-investment period. Obviously, patience can prove a virtue *after* you have made an investment, too, although my experience is that a Board and a management team that doesn't exhibit a constant sense of urgency is unlikely to produce above average results. But patience is crucial with respect to the discipline of *not* investing, of being able to

say no, and of waiting for the right opportunities to come along.

16 *A well-structured shareholders agreement never needs to come out of your desk.* A venture capitalist can do much to protect his or her minority status with a sensibly written shareholders agreement. Such an agreement can also avoid unnecessary disputation and wasted energy for all parties if it deals with conflict resolution, exit timetables and procedure, hiring/firing of key executives, capital expenditure limits and other such key business issues.

17 *Don't be greedy!* You will never go broke leaving something on the table for the next guy; you will come a cropper one day if you try to catch the peak of the market every time you exit a deal. And if you try to price your companies' IPOs too high, the investors won't be there for the next one.

18 *Think globally, not parochially, when it comes to exit time.* Taking a company to an IPO offshore should not be regarded as un-Australian. By arranging access for the company to the most suitable capital markets, onshore or offshore, the venture capitalist will minimise the company's cost of capital while maximising shareholder values. Squandering or delaying the commercial exploitation of Australian inventiveness is what must be avoided in the national interest.

19 *With acquisitions, 1 plus 1 sometimes equals less than 2.* Assumptions about economies of scale, about the benefits from horizontal or vertical integration, about dividends from technology transfer, sometimes remain just that . . . assumptions. Frequently, I have seen the enthusiasm for growth by acquisition run ahead of thorough analysis. This results, more often than not, in damage to the offer or a diluting of the very strength of the core proposition that attracted you in the first place.

20 *Never make an investment without first having an explicit agreement with the investee company's owners about the exit process and timetable.* Getting out can be a lot harder than getting in. When the time is appropriate to sell, venture capitalists need to be able to move efficiently and in harmony with others involved. Entrepreneurs and founders often, and understandably, fall in love with their companies; their time horizons may shift and diverge significantly from those of the venture capitalists.

reflections

Looking back over the investments described in this book, good and not so good, and reflecting on my three decades in venture capital, I ask myself the obvious question: what would I do differently?

The answer is, there's probably not very much. In 1970 there were no role models or 'how to' manuals, but even if I'd had prior knowledge of the lessons outlined in this book there would surely have been other mistakes, other misadventures—and other adventures. One thing is certain, I would do it all again and pursue a life and career in venture capital.

Thinking about my experiences, though, I keep coming back to a particular issue.

A recent discussion in venture capital circles, in the United States in particular, suggests that market timing may be all-important, more important than the people involved in the deal. It has been traditional for venture capitalists to stress that the most important elements in an investment decision and its outcome are people, people, people—rather like the real estate developer's maxim that the three most important things are position, position, position.

More recently still, some of the outstanding Sandhill Road venture capitalists in Silicon Valley, like John Doerr of Kleiner, Perkins, Caulfield & Byers, have concluded that, with an accelerated rate of innovation in electronics and information technology, deals won't work even with talented people with exemplary track records if the market goes past you. With successes like Sun Microsystems, Compaq, Lotus, Netscape and Cisco to his name, John Doerr has impressive credentials. He and other venture capitalists argue that if you have the right product or idea at the right time in the market cycle you can always find the right people to execute the business plan. I suspect that this view may be more valid in the United States, with its vast depth of entrepreneurs and executives, than it is in a smaller market economy such as Australia.

Of course, when a sector is on the boil, like the internet in 1998 and 1999, it is tempting to conclude that just being in the river of dot com companies is better than standing on the river bank searching for experienced internet boatmen to ride with, especially when a voracious IPO market is calling for more dot coms and providing the venture capitalists with quick exit opportunities.

But in the light of my own experiences I feel that, if I had to choose between a wonderful market opportunity and a wonderful entrepreneur, I would still take the entrepreneur every time. Perhaps this is because I am lazy. Of course, whether you are in the United States or in Australia, the great market opportunity and the wonderful entrepreneur are not mutually exclusive—you hope they co-exist. Like Rothwell and his Austal fast ferries, Thornley and his LookSmart category-driven search engine, or Herrick and his 'Made in France' varietal wines.

My experience has been that, in the long run, the right entrepreneur will always make you money. He will dig you out of a hole, he will be there on Sundays when necessary and he will out-punch the other guys because he wants it all so badly.

I had an opportunity to interview General Georges Doriot back in 1970. Doriot was the founding president of American

Research & Development Corporation (ARD), the pioneer venture capital company in the US. He was a remarkable Frenchman who was a Harvard Business School professor in manufacturing. I met him during my time at Harvard when I was looking for ideas and assistance in establishing a venture capital company in Australia.

ARD received front page attention in the late sixties when Doriot's $100 000 investment in Digital Equipment Corporation turned into $400 million at the time of its New York Stock Exchange listing.

What was the key to the success of this extraordinary company? 'Unquestionably its CEO, Ken Olsen,' Doriot replied in his delightful French American accent.

Doriot told me that Digital was formed to produce computer peripherals and was doing so quite adequately. One night he received a call from Olsen with an invitation to have a drink with him at home. Here he discovered that Olsen had been building a mini-computer in the basement of his home after hours. This mini was to ultimately challenge IBM and the paradigm of mainframe computing.

And what was the single most important characteristic exhibited by this outstanding CEO? Doriot thought quietly for several minutes and then said, 'Ken's sustained attention to detail over several years.' This was not the answer I was expecting about a man with Olsen's breakthrough vision as to how computing could be miniaturised. I suppose that is why the answer has remained so clearly in my mind.

Perhaps Victor Hugo makes the point more elegantly when, in *Les Miserables*, he describes genius as 'a creature with a telescope in one eye and a microscope in the other, rummaging about in the infinitely large and the infinitely small'.

Doriot's response was instructive for me. Maybe you think it's a bit folksy and old-fashioned—maybe. But I can tell you that each and every one of the successful CEOs featured in this book also exhibits this characteristic.

part TWO

We sail into the ancient port of Knidos just before lunch on a beautiful blue and calm Aegean day. It is still June and not too hot. Knidos lies several hours south from the much larger port of Bodrum on the Turkish coast. Knidos is framed by splendid hills on two sides and there's an isthmus at its end where the Aegean actually meets the Mediterranean. It is a safe and wonderfully interesting anchorage.

As our eyes focus on the hillside we realise that we are surrounded by the ancient ruins of what must have been a thriving and cultured civilisation. At the water's edge, in a prime position like Sydney's Opera House, rests a splendid amphitheatre still in good condition.

What also draws me to Knidos is my curiosity about an extraordinary venture capital project launched by the city officials some 2400 years ago. In those days Knidos actively competed with nearby ports for the custom and trade of all sorts of shipping. The city grew famous for its shops, its theatres and its professional women; it attracted fishermen, merchants and navy vessels from far and wide.

To further enhance its position, the officials commissioned a massive sculpture of the beautiful Aphrodite, to be erected in the temple of Apollo high above the urban centre. It was an expensive project. Would it work, would the returns be there, and how long before one got one's money back? Questions the venture capitalist is always wrestling with.

Aphrodite was the first known nude statue of a woman and caused instant and considerable controversy. Like it or hate it, you had to come and see it. And so it proved to be a big success—at least until the scandal of the nude goddess brought such disrepute upon the city that the sculpture mysteriously went missing. Today only its impressive round marble base remains and, alas, no trace of the nude has yet been discovered. Nonetheless, the legend of this high risk, high risqué venture lives on.

Back in the cockpit after an exhausting hike to the site of the missing Aphrodite, my mind drifts back to our own much shorter history of venture capital in Australia. And so to Part Two.

development of venture capital activity in australia

The financing of voyages such as Captain Cook's in *Endeavour* in 1768–71 was quintessential venture capital—high risk money funding uncertain journeys of discovery, perhaps with treasure and booty in return, perhaps with wrecks, lost lives and total loss of capital. This was 'gutsy' venture capitalism on the part of the British Admiralty and the British Treasury of the day.

The subsequent settlement of Australia in 1788 is in a way an even more remarkable venture capital project. Transportation of prisoners seemed like a brilliant and cheap solution at the time for an impossibly overcrowded and expensive prison system in London. The jettisoning of prisoners to an offshore facility was an imaginative solution, rendered possible by British maritime technology and seamanship. Yet the British soon learned that they had a tiger by the tail when the costs of building a settlement in faraway Sydney dramatically outpaced any revenue generation. Decades were to pass before innovations such as Merino wool and gold discoveries reversed the cash drain on the British Treasury.

It has been said that necessity is the mother of invention. The special requirements for survival in a harsh geography and climate, remote from external solutions, not surprisingly produced a culture of self-sufficiency and inventiveness among early settlers in Australia.

Whitehall had prohibited the building of boats in the colonics, sincc such vcssels wcrc considcrcd potcntial instrumcnts of escape. However, in the best New South Wales tradition, the local authorities turned a blind eye to the entrepreneurial craftsmen who by 1805 had built an amazing 40 vessels. These vessels were essential to the expansion of sealing, whaling and trading and to meet the demand of new settlements along the Hawkesbury and Parramatta rivers. This innovative maritime tradition has since produced other remarkable seagoing achievements for Australia, including Ben Lexcen's America's Cup winning winged-keel design, and a world-leading industry of high speed ferry design and construction led by INCAT in Hobart, Tasmania, and Austal in Perth, Western Australia.

The 'tyranny of distance' also spurred James Harrison to invent the world's first ice-making machine, allowing the start of a meat export trade in 1857. Of similar impact to the agribusiness prospects of the Australian economy was the stump-jump plough. Invented by Robert Smith in South Australia during 1876, this clever mechanical innovation allowed crop production on terrain previously too rough to be economical.

These and other innovations combined with the blood, sweat and tears of convicts and settlers to eventually reverse the

Australian 'cash burn' into a surplus for the British. Their bold investment in Australia produced hardearned venture capital style returns—eventually!

It was to be at least another 100 years, however, before an Australian-based venture capital industry took shape. Before attempting a description of this more recent history I should first say a little more on what is meant by the term 'venture capital'.

The US National Venture Capital Association defines it as: 'Capital provided by firms of full-time professionals who invest alongside management in young, rapidly growing or changing companies that have the potential to develop into significant competitors in regional, national or global markets.' Venture capital activities involve more than just the provision of funding, and include the active participation and involvement of the investors in the management and strategic focus of the business. Essential to the concept of venture capital is the fact that investors provide equity, rather than debt, to the investee. Venture capital generally does not include investments into the asset classes of property or capital-intensive projects such as mineral extraction.

Chris Golis includes a useful description in his instructive book, *Enterprise and Venture Capital* (3rd edition, Allen & Unwin, Sydney, 1998). He writes:

> Simply put, *venture capital may be regarded as an equity investment where investors expect significant capital gains in return for accepting the risk they may lose all their equity.* Typically, the investment is either in a privately held company or a publicly listed company that has just started and does not have a track record of producing dividends for investors. The other major form of venture capital investment is in the leveraged buyout of stable, mature businesses. Here the buyout is financed with a larger than usual proportion of debt, placing the equity component in a correspondingly riskier position.

Venture capital investments may be made at different stages of a businesses life cycle, including the following:

- *Seed investing* Investing in an idea, before the formation of the company or development of any product.

- *Early-stage investing* Capital provided to a company in its first stages of development.
- *Expansion-stage funding* Funding to help already established firms to accelerate their expansion into existing or new markets; to prepare them for subsequent listing on a stock exchange; or to prepare them for sale or for merger with other companies.
- *Management buy-outs buy-ins* Funding advanced to assist the acquisition of a business by an existing or a new management team. This usually involves the acquisition of an established, often mature, enterprise with equity provided by the venture capitalist and debt of up to 75 per cent of the transaction value supplied by senior and subordinate lenders (usually banks). In these transactions the venture capitalist acts as the control investor with 80–90 per cent of the shareholding, the management team holding the balance.

The normal length of a venture capital investment is 3–5 years, and the normal duration of a fund is around ten years.

1945 to 1970

Prior to the emergence of dedicated professional venture fund managers in the 1970s, private capital was supplied from time to time in post–World War II Australia by wealthy private investors. This occurred predominantly in the form of family support for private family-run businesses. No formal market for private capital, as such, existed.

Then, during the 1960s, venture capital was tapped by the public markets in the form of public subscription to a plethora of mineral and oil exploration companies. The companies were speculative explorers and many of their public share issues were rendered popular by various income tax deductions then available. These tax schemes were driven by a government policy aimed at achieving development of the capital-hungry resources sector, with maximum Australian ownership.

In the early 1960s Australia experienced a huge surge in the minerals sector, with spectacular 'boom and bust' stock market performances. Companies such as the nickel explorer, Poseidon, experienced share price movements and valuation templates reminiscent of today's publicly traded internet companies. In a period of less than twelve months, Poseidon shares ran from $10 each to $260; within another twelve months they were less than $1.

There is no analysis available to me which objectively measures the cost/benefits of the tax-driven government intervention, but my estimate is that the ore discoveries and their subsequent development probably justified the exploration costs and the tax deductions that accompanied these costs. This was a sector-specific venture capital experience which evaporated with the removal of the tax schemes and with the burst bubble of the speculative minerals market boom.

Later on in the 1960s another sector-specific and tax-driven venture capital activity occurred. This time it was based on a public policy aimed at stimulating the development of an Australian film industry. My business partner, Joe Skrzynski, was then very active in that industry and is regarded as the father of the '10BA tax deduction scheme'—tax legislation providing incentives for investors in film production. A significant flow of risk capital was stimulated primarily from wealthy individual investors; between 1968 and 1978 a number of films such as *Sunday Too Far Away*, *Gallipoli* and *Picnic at Hanging Rock* put a fledgling Australian movie industry on the world screen. Of course, there were many failures too in what has traditionally been something of a hit or miss business.

The politics of this sector-specific support shifted by the late 1970s when the taxation incentives had largely been removed. Nonetheless, an industry had been kickstarted; Australian directors, producers, actors, writers and cameramen have since continued to build a worldwide reputation for the Australian film industry.

These spurts of sector-specific venture capitalism did not, however, lead to the formation of venture capital funds as such, and it was not until 1970 that venture capital management companies began to emerge.

1970 to 1984

The first Australian venture capital company, International Venture Corporation Pty Ltd (IVC), was founded by me in August 1970. Capitalised with less than $500 000, the shareholders, apart from myself, included David Stone of Boston, Rod Carnegie and Baillieu Myer of Melbourne, Evelyn de Rothschild of London, and various private investors from Sydney including John Walton, Rodney Hudspeth, Gary Bogard, Nick Whitlam and the O'Neil family. American Research & Development Inc. and Memorial Drive Trust (the investment arm of the Arthur D. Little Group) were also early shareholders from the United States.

Two years later, Hill Samuel Australia (later to become the Macquarie Bank) acquired approximately 25 per cent in IVC and Macquarie's David Clarke joined the Board. The Board now comprised Bryan Kelman as chairman, myself as managing director, Ted Vogt representing Textron Inc. (the then owner of AR&D), David Clarke, Rodney O'Neil and Gary Bogard (a former partner in the law firm, Freehill Hollingdale and Page).

IVC was the first venture firm established in Australia dedicated to private capital transactions. Early investments included businesses in aquaculture, road surfacing and concrete, consumer finance and leasing, property services, marine equipment manufacturing, intensive piggeries, offpeak heater manufacturing, Australian film production, laser equipment, minerals exploration and pyrophillite extraction and processing.

At that time Joe Skrzynski was in charge of Finance Facilities Pty Ltd, the non-property business activities of Sir Paul Strasser. Finance Facilities provided investment support to a number of unlisted entities. These included the first business in licensed taverns, a firm making safety car seats for babies, a chemical coatings enterprise and several others.

Within two years of IVC's commencement another venture firm was formed by Dr Timothy Pascoe, who was managing director. Shareholders included Rod Carnegie and Bails Myer from Melbourne and Chris Abbott from Sydney; the initial capitalisation was approximately $1 million. This company was called Enterprise Management of Australia Corporation (EMA) and investments were completed in the tourism and leisure sector, manufacturing and services. An early success was a transaction backing John Elliott in the acquisition of the IXL jam enterprise.

Like IVC, EMA experienced mixed results in the early years and the Board decided to sell off investments and return proceeds. IVC did likewise in the early 1980s, including a distribution in specie in the successful Barlow Marine portfolio company.

Another early player in the private capital sector was John Grant who, in the late 1970s, opened a venture capital management business with the sponsorship of Hambros Bank in Australia. This business has continued under the name of Hambro-Grantham, with a focus on small technology companies. Grant was successful in obtaining a licence under the Management and Investment Companies (MIC) scheme referred to below, and in establishing a parallel fund.

In the late 1970s, one or two other initiatives appeared, including a company called Australian Innovation Corporation. It was formed to invest only in very early-stage ventures and found the going too tough, with disappointing financial results.

Another institutional player that then emerged was the government-owned AIDC, Australian Industry Development Corporation. Focused primarily on major manufacturing and mining project financing, the AIDC also included private equity transactions among its activities. This provided it with some solid results in the wine and mineral processing sectors during the late 1970s and early 1980s. It also had an outstanding financial success in the 1980s in the Australian Submarine Corporation, building submarines in partnership with Kockums of Sweden. The AIDC's record in smaller high technology investing was, at best, mixed. Successes included Paul Trainor's pioneering medical instruments company, Nucleus. The AIDC was a patient and brave long-term investor in Nucleus, eventually achieving outstanding profits from its investment when the company was acquired by Pacific Dunlop. The AIDC's investment in Optus was also ultimately a profitable experience.

However, many other AIDC investments in computer manufacturers, telecoms equipment suppliers, software development companies and a variety of specialty retailers all proved unsuccessful. These failures forced its pullback from private capital investing in the late 1980s.

Following the lead of the Federal Government, and in response to the politics of the day, several State governments also established investment funds to promote their domestic industries. The major ones were the Victorian Development Corporation, the West Australian Development Authority, the Queensland-based Venture Fund and the South Australian-based Enterprise Investments. Most State funds were launched in the mid-1970s and held equity investments in small scale businesses, typically investing \$0.5–\$2 million. The success of these funds was highly variable and most were badly affected by the 1987 stock market crash. All except for the Victorian Investment Corporation have downsized or have been wound up since the early 1990s. State governments today attempt to promote industries in different ways, such as sponsoring technology incubators and encouraging domestic investment from interstate and international IT companies to provide skills and spinoff technologies to the local industry.

Another important institutional effort was led by the National Australia Bank in partnership with Charterhouse from Britain and the A.C. Goode brokerage house. This company was formed as a venture capital business and was staffed by 'experts' from Britain. Called Paternoster Partners, it proved unsuccessful and was liquidated within five years or so. It was to be almost 20 years before the NAB re-entered the venture capital market.

The experience of these pioneers in the first ten to fifteen years leading up to the MIC licence program in 1984 was at best mixed. Some portfolio company successes like Barlow Marine, IXL, Nucleus and others demonstrated that venture capital could indeed work in Australia. Overall, however, the financial returns to investors did not prove compelling enough to shift the attitudes of a still risk-averse institutional investment sector. If anything, the early returns entrenched the 'I told you so' attitude in the boardrooms of the major banks and superannuation funds around the country. Australians, it seemed, were willing risk takers on the weekends at the racetrack, but from Monday to Friday the boardrooms were decidedly risk-averse. Banks were asset-backing lenders, not cash flow financiers. They were interested in real estate property, not intellectual property. Similarly, the major superannuation fund managers achieved sound enough returns for their superannuants by investing in the top 100 public companies, government securities and inflation-driven real estate. Why should they take the extra risks involved in private capital transactions? Indeed, superannuation fund trustees had onerous responsibilities to their members and could be held liable for investment losses.

It was not until the end of the 1980s that legislation defining the responsibilities of trustees was altered such that trustees could allocate a percentage of their portfolio to various risk categories without being individually responsible for any specific investment loss within any one such risk category.

It was against this background that inquiries were established by Federal Government. The Crawford study group on structural adjustment in 1979 recommended the creation of an Australian Innovation Authority; the Myers Committee inquiry into technological change in 1980 also recommended government involvement in increasing the supply of venture capital. The Ferris Committee report in 1984, entitled *Lifting the Performance of Manufacturing and Services Exports*, recommended venture capital assistance for high technology exporters.

Various submissions were made to these inquiries by those of us active in the industry at that time, and also to the 1983 Campbell report on the Australian financial system.

1984 to 1990

The Espie Committee had been established in 1981 to 'consider and report on the problems facing high technology enterprises in Australia'. Its 1983 report identified several factors inhibiting the supply of venture capital in Australia, including:

- an apparent lack of quality management, particularly in high technology industries
- poor attitudes towards investment in high-risk, long-term investments, whose appeal was not as great as that of short-term, risk-averse investments
- Australia's lack of technology development, partly as a result of the lack of capital, and also because of tight government controls of many IT industry players, such as Telecom (now Telstra) and the CSIRO
- the failure of government to support small businesses by means of assisting venture capitalists.

The Espie report recommended that the government be the catalyst in developing a venture capital base domestically, by offering incentives to encourage investment in small businesses. Acting on this, the government established the Management and Investment Companies (MIC) scheme to take advantage of the perceived opportunities that developing high technology companies were offering in terms of wealth creation and economic growth.

A strong champion for government intervention in the venture capital markets at that time was the Minister for Industry, The Honourable John Button. Button was well respected for his industry development work over many years. He had resisted cries for legislation to compel the superannuation funds to allocate some percentage of their capital into venture activities. While acknowledging that a 'market failure' did exist in the early stage funding market, he did not believe that a compulsory investment scheme would work in Australia politically or commercially.

He was, however, prepared to try a more limited intervention, hence the MIC program was born.

The MIC program was implemented in 1984 to encourage and promote investment in innovative startup technology businesses, by offering financial, strategic and administrative assistance to venture capital investors. The government did this through the issuing of a limited number of MIC licences to companies that could satisfy the government's strict criteria.

The licensees, listed in Table 8, raised almost $400 million.

Table 8

Company or fund	Fund size ($m)
Austech Ventures Ltd	27.5
Australian Pacific Technology Ltd	29.4
BT Innovation Ltd	22.5
Continental Venture Capital Ltd	95.1
Corporate Enterprise Investments Ltd	0.2
CP Ventures Ltd	40.4
First MIC Ltd	52.4
Greenchip Opportunities Ltd	13.7
Japan Australia Venture Capital Fund	8.3
Samic Ltd	15.9
Stinoc Ltd	26.4
Techniche Ltd	19.3
Western Pacific Investment Company Ltd	29.0
Westintech Innovation Corporation Ltd	11.7

Table 9 shows the annual performance of the overall MIC scheme, in terms of the amount raised and where the proceeds were directed.

Table 9

Year	Amount raised	Amount invested	Number of new investee businesses
1983/84	Combined with 1984–85	0.1	1
1984/85	79.1	8.5	19
1985/86	41.0	35.5	47
1986/87	69.3	53.3	47
1987/88	40.7	45.7	25
1988/89	15.7	31.8	9
1989/90	58.6	39.1	5
1990/91	87.5	11.3	2
Total	**392.1**	**225.4**	**155**

Note: Totals may differ due to rounding errors
Source: Management and Investment Companies Licensing Board, Annual Report 1988/89

During the scheme's eight year life the fourteen licensed fund managers invested in over 150 companies. By the termination of the scheme, the entire venture capital market consisted of 32 different funds with a capital base of $794 million.

Certain of these licensees established 'parallel funds' which effectively leveraged the MIC scheme further by attracting the involvement of a number of institutional investors. Some of the early parallel funds launched by MIC companies were:

- Advent Western Pacific parallel fund, managed by Western Pacific Investment Co.
- Melbourne Australia Investments parallel fund, managed by Continental Venture Capital Co.
- H-G Ventures parallel fund, managed by First MIC Ltd.

By the end of 1986 the MIC program had achieved apparent moderate success, largely buoyed by investor confidence and strong growth in the overall economy. However, the October 1987 stock market crash destroyed equity markets worldwide. Following the huge losses for many large entrepreneurs and super funds, market enthusiasm for private equity waned. In addition, the impact of the crash meant that most of the MIC funds' existing investments required additional financing, which restricted the amount of capital available to other potential investments.

The scheme never recovered from the blow of 1987 and the disappearance of the Second Boards on the stock exchanges.

With the benefit of hindsight, the architecture of the MIC scheme was fundamentally flawed. The upfront tax deduction led to a separation of ownership and control of the funds; the incentive was realised by tax-driven investors regardless of the investment outcomes. Furthermore, the restrictions on how the money could be invested virtually guaranteed future failure. Only investments in early-stage technology companies were permitted; since a maximum investment for most MIC funds was only about $1 million in any one investee, most of the MICs developed extremely high risk portfolios with no capacity for follow-on support investing.

Nonetheless, several successful investees emerged, including Cochlear, AMRAD, ISP and Vision Systems. In addition, teams of young executives entered the industry and 'cut their teeth'; many of these executives remain in the industry today. In this sense, the MIC program was an invaluable step along the way to creating today's viable and profitable venture capital industry.

Secondary sharemarkets, called Second Boards, were established in Australia by all State-run stock exchanges—led by Perth in July 1984. Prima facie, a Second Board was beneficial to venture capitalists as it provided an exit mechanism for investors to realise their investments in cases where a firm had developed but was not established enough to list on the Main Board. The Second Board was also popular with business owners for its more favourable listing requirements, such as permitting companies with different share classes to list. This enabled small business owners to retain control of their business after listing, even if they were not the senior shareholder. Second Boards were not without their undesirable attributes, however, with many businesses listing prematurely relative to their stage of development. The Second Board companies were too small to warrant the attention of investment research analysis and the major institutional investors were disinterested or unable to invest.

By October 1987, 243 companies had listed on Australian Second Boards, having collectively raised $1.4 billion and achieved a market capitalisation of $3.8 billion. In terms of share performance, Second Board companies significantly outperformed the Main Board in the three years leading to March 1987 and their success was buoyed by the growth of the economy. As with the MIC funds, all Second Boards were devastated by the drying up of capital and the increased risk-aversion of investors following the 1987 crash, and eventually they all became redundant.

Corporate venturing also emerged in the 1980s and was attempted by firms such as Amcor, Telstra, BHP and CRA, which typically invested in firms relevant to their own areas of industry. Large corporations tended to invest in venture capital either by allocating funds to internal fund managers, by establishing subsidiary venture capital companies, or by investing in independent venture companies. On the whole, these efforts did not prove very successful.

A more recent entrant in the Australian corporate venturing field is Acer Computers, through its establishment of a $30 million fund for investment in smaller Australian computer companies. Intel also has recently made an allocation to Australia as part of its worldwide venture investing strategy.

The Federal Government has provided many other incentives to small- and medium-size enterprises over the years, typically to encourage investment in the areas of exporting and R&D. In July 1985 the government introduced its R&D concession scheme, which offered a 150 per cent tax concession for businesses whose annual R&D expenditure exceeds $50 000 annually.

The Grants for Industry Research and Development (GIRD) scheme was introduced to complement the R&D concession scheme by further encouraging a focus on new and emerging technologies. Three different grants were available, depending on the importance of the investment to both the company and the Australian economy. These were in the form of discretionary grants for small, high technology firms; generic technology grants for new and emerging technologies fundamental to industry competitiveness; and National Interest Agreements for R&D projects that created national benefits.

Following the Ferris Committee report in 1984, the High Technology Exporters scheme was introduced by the government in 1986 to improve the export performance of appropriate companies. Eligible companies could qualify for export industry assistance if they could demonstrate funding support from the AIDC or from an MIC licensee.

The National Industry Extension Service (NIES) was a Commonwealth and State collaboration to aid in the delivery of information, referral and diagnostic services to the industry, and was launched in March 1987. NIES attempted to encourage firms to modernise their management and production systems, with the overall intention of increasing efficiency and competitiveness in local industry.

In 1987, Joe Skrzynski and I came together to form Australian Mezzanine Investments Pty Limited (AMIL) with the ambition of building Australia's pre-eminent private capital funds management group. Our first fund, AMIT No. 1, was subscribed by a small number of institutional investors with a total amount of $30 million.

In mid-1987, Joe and I had suggested to our potential backers that the stock market was looking over-heated and a market correction would likely occur. Such a correction, we argued, would assist our efforts since smaller companies would no longer find such easy (and, in our view, premature) access to the then over-priced public equities markets.

However, we had not expected the stock market collapse of October 1987. Following this market rout, we provided all our investors with the opportunity to reconsider their commitments to AMIT No. 1; to their credit, and our considerable gratitude, only one of the five pulled out.

Not long after, and under the auspices of Bond Street Investments Pty Ltd, Macquarie Bank indicated its intention to expand its private equities business. With David Clarke as its chairman and the popular, plain-talking Sandy Lockhart as its chief executive, Bond Street later became Macquarie Direct Investment Management with its first fund, the Macquarie Investment Trust No. 1, subscribed to $51 million early in 1988. Macquarie has continued to successfully expand its activities to be one of the best-performing private capital managers in Australia today.

1990 to 1999

Pooled Development Funds The MIC program was officially replaced by the Pooled Development Funds (PDF) program, which was announced in the Federal Government's 1992 Economic Statement. This program aims to improve the access of small- and medium-size enterprises to domestic private equity, by offering registered PDFs tax concessions and other investment incentives. The PDF program was introduced in an attempt to remove some of the problems inherent in the unsuccessful MIC scheme, such as lack of flexibility and absence of incentive to institutional investors. A significant tax incentive provided to investors has been the exemption from capital gains tax on any sale of shares by investors in a PDF. To satisfy the PDF program, funds have to abide by a number of regulations.

The flexibility of the *Pooled Development Funds Act 1992* has allowed changes in the program to occur and several of these have helped to promote the scheme since its inception. In 1994 improved tax incentives were offered to allow the distribution of dividends to be either tax exempt or applied to a dividend imputation system. This change attempted to further encourage investors, in particular superannuation funds, to invest in PDFs, for which the tax benefits were previously negligible due to existing tax regulations. The continual registration of new funds has intensified competition among fund managers and has increased the overall pool of available capital. As a result, rapid growth in PDF capital raising and investment has occurred, despite difficulties in attracting overseas investment due to prohibitive tax regulations.

In 1998 the PDF Act was again amended and, for the first time, the government permitted share buy-back schemes to increase the liquidity of the investments for investors. The amendments also allowed super funds to fully own PDFs so as to further encourage domestic and overseas super fund participation—where previously they could own only up to 30 per cent. Additional changes enabled PDFs to offer loans to a maximum of 20 per cent of their capital base, where previously loans could not be made at all. PDFs were also permitted to merge, as long as cash was not paid out by either PDF in the course of such a merger.

To July 1998, 66 registered PDFs had invested over $155 million from a total pool of raised capital of $279 million. Table 10 gives the details.

Table 10

Year	*Amount raised during year ($m)*	*Cumulative amount raised ($m)*	*Number of PDFs*	*Cumulative number of investee companies*
1992/93	20	20	5	0
1993/94	15	35	11	37
1994/95	26	61	26	59
1995/96	74	135	40	89
1996/97	29	164	51	120
1997/98	115	279	66	147

Source: Pooled Development Funds Registration Board, *Annual Report: The Pooled Development Funds Program*, AGPS, Canberra, 1994–98

To date, the impact of PDFs on the venture capital industry has been modest, both in terms of capital raisings and investee performance. The regulatory restrictions on the activities of PDFs have contributed to this outcome, including the inability of PDFs to invest in large companies or in foreign-owned entities. Nonetheless, the PDFs have deepened the venture capital markets and can be expected to continue to do so, especially if various recommendations of the Ralph Committee of Inquiry are adopted in 2000.

Co-operative Research Centres Historically, Australia has punched well above its weight in terms of scientific breakthroughs. However, it has also punched below its weight in terms of commercialisation of breakthroughs. Its contributions to penicillin, x-ray crystallography, xerography (forerunner of Xerox), the black box flight recorder and many other world firsts have been commercialised by others.

In response to the 1989 ASTEC report, *The Core Capacity of Australian Science and Technology*, which recommended the development of interdisciplinary science and research centres, the Federal Government established the Co-operative Research Centre (CRC) program in May 1990. The program aims to bring together public sector bodies, higher education institutions and industry, through the formation of large and integrated teams, in order to facilitate specialised research. The specific objectives of the program are to:

- contribute to economic and social development and the establishment of internationally competitive industry sectors through support for long-term, high quality research
- commercialise the benefits of research
- increase skills through training and education of graduates and researchers
- promote the efficient use of R&D by strengthening research networks and building specific centres to conduct research.

There have been five selection rounds since the program's launch in 1990 and, although early CRCs were heavily government-funded, the private sector has become increasingly involved.

Since 1991, 67 CRCs have been established across Australia, in the following areas:

- manufacturing technology
- information and communication technology
- mining and energy
- agriculture and related industries
- environment
- medical science and technology.

The impressive range of CRCs is evident in the full list set out in the Appendix.

CRCs are generally established under contracts that run for seven years. They are selected by the Minister for Industry, Science and Resources on the advice of the selection committee, which in turn is advised by expert panels. Since the establishment of the first CRC in 1991, the government has committed over $1.1 billion to the program, with other CRC partners having committed $2.7 billion, including $640 million from industry. The government has outlaid an average of $140 million annually to support the program, providing between 16 per cent and 49 per cent of the funding to the Centres. A 1997 review concluded that CRCs represent an effective investment of public funds and that a majority of the Centres have been beneficial in encouraging innovation and change.

Although not intended to be profitable entities, some CRCs have generated external earnings, primarily through providing contract research. In 1996/97 this amounted to $46 million, which represented an increase of $11 million compared with the funds earned in 1995/96. Participation in the program has also grown dramatically and currently includes over 250 Australian and international companies, 61 State government departments and agencies, 35 universities, 24 CSIRO divisions, eight Commonwealth research agencies, eight rural R&D corporations and numerous other organisations.

An example of a successful Centre is the Australian Photonics CRC, which brings together the Universities of New South Wales, Sydney and Melbourne, the Australian National University, and industry players including Telstra and Siemens. The CRC co-ordinates over 80 per cent of R&D in photonics communications and, since 1991, has enabled telecommunications firms to increase the capacity of optical fibre networks by a factor of ten! The success of this CRC led to an extension in funding to further support the technology, with eight additional partners joining the program in 1997. Two years earlier, in 1995, the CRC founders established a startup company, Indx, at the Australian Technology Park in Sydney. Indx has won several major contracts, including a deal with Fujitsu to supply optical cable to link Europe and the South Pacific.

Co-operative Research Centres will almost certainly prove to be a growing source of products and ideas for the venture capital market in future years. The test of commercial relevance that the industry participants bring to CRC priorities will very likely produce a marked improvement in the rate of commercialisation of Australian scientific breakthroughs.

START scheme In April 1997 Prime Minister Howard, in his Small Business statement, officially approved the START scheme, an investment encouragement program with five major components, one of which specifically targets the venture capital industry and is called the Innovation Investment Fund (IIF). The IIF was established to complement the Pooled Development Funds program and is a major AusIndustry initiative designed to encourage the commercialisation of Australian high technology companies by matching every dollar privately raised with two dollars from the government. The IIF specifically targets technology companies and attempts to fill the void left by venture capitalists focusing on developed businesses, rather than emerging and startup investments. The initiative followed extensive consultation with the Australian Venture Capital Association and a review of similar programs in the United States, Israel and elsewhere.

Provision of incentives to private sector investors to bother with the higher risks and costs involved in early-stage technology investments is basic to the aims of the IIF. Lessons drawn from the earlier MIC scheme led to a much improved architecture for the incentives provided. Rewarding actual achievement at the back end rather than providing tax deductions upfront and requiring private money to actually be at risk alongside the government funds were two important improvements.

A fund's life is expected to be ten years, with a minimum of half the capital being invested in seed, startup or first round funding. In return for its provision of funds, the government requires repayment of capital plus the bond yield plus 10 per cent of the profits of the investments. Under the initial proposal, $130 million in funding has been committed by the government on a two for one matching basis with approved venture capital managers, thereby creating $195 million for new technology company investments.

The IIF program is an innovative move and represents the most significant government initiative taken to encourage early-stage investment since the MIC scheme in 1984. The amount committed to the program has made the government the largest single investor in the early-stage venture capital industry and has been a successful step towards re-establishing a venture capital industry geared to provision of startup and early-stage capital.

In December 1997, five companies were allocated licences under the IIF. These were Allen & Buckeridge Investment Management, AMWIN Management (a joint venture between Australian Mezzanine Investments and the Walden International Investment Group), Coates Myer & Co., Rothschild Bioscience Managers and Momentum Funds Management.

The other components of AusIndustry's R&D START scheme support business research and development by providing grants and loans to firms. The government initiative pledged to provide $700 million over four years (from 1998) for small- and medium-size enterprises (SMEs) to undertake industry R&D and related activities. The four other components are as follows:

1 *Core Start* provides assistance of up to 50 per cent of project costs through grants and loans for R&D-based investments by SMEs

2 *Start Plus* targets larger businesses and offers up to 20 per cent of project costs for firms with a group turnover exceeding $50 million

3 *Start Premium* provides a repayable amount of up to 56.25 per cent of project costs and is intended for high quality research projects

4 *Start Graduate* grants are awarded to companies with revenues under $50 million to employ a graduate to undertake R&D-related research in collaboration with a research institution for up to two years.

All of the grants are offered to support R&D projects in Australia for up to three years, with grants being given on a competitive basis. In R&D START's first round of funding in April 1997, sixteen projects were offered a total of $44 million.

To some extent these various research-based programs have 'politically' replaced the previous R&D syndicate investment programs, which were brought into disrepute by a preoccupation with rewards to investors from the excellence of financial engineering rather than the excellence of the science funded.

Other schemes Another government-inspired initiative in venture capital was the Keating Government's establishment of the Australian Multimedia Enterprise (AME) in 1995 as part of its 'Creative Nation' policy. AME was to provide $45 million for investment in multimedia projects and concept developments, with the primary focus being directed towards CD-ROMs and online services. AME's aim was both to promote the growth of technology companies domestically and to provide research and literature on the status and nature of technology-based industries in Australia. By 1998 it had funded more than 90 Australian projects, benefiting over 300 practitioners. However, throughout its government-owned life, the scheme was the subject of constant criticism for not having outlaid anywhere near as much of the $45 million as it had initially pledged.

AME was sold to Allen & Buckeridge in April 1997, having invested $15 million in various projects. Earlier in that year, the government reclaimed $16 million in a share capital return from AME, and reclaimed a further $13.3 million from Allen

& Buckeridge in a share buy-back following the sale. The government justified the sale of AME by claiming that the Innovation Investment Fund was larger and better targeted at startup companies.

Following the failure of the Second Boards during the 1980s, the Australian Stock Exchange (ASX) again attempted to show its commitment to growing businesses by establishing the Enterprise Market in April 1998. This Internet-based business introduction service aimed to facilitate capital raising for Australia's estimated 10 000 SMEs which, in 1998, were seeking an estimated $5 billion in funding through a single national market for non-listed businesses. The service targets 'business angels', or wealthy private investors, who might otherwise not be informed of potential business opportunities. The Enterprise Market enables firms to list company information online and it attempts to work with existing business introduction services to create a single 'business angel' market in Australia, as is the case in the United States.

A Yellow Pages survey of small business revealed that, in 1997, business angels invested in excess of $1 billion in 6800 businesses, and the angels are becoming an increasingly important source of finance for startup and early-stage companies.

'Incubators' are another approach. They are State government initiatives to create mini–Silicon Valleys, which bring developing high technology companies and resources together in order to provide the wherewithal—resources, knowledge, skills and so on—needed to facilitate collective growth of the tenant firms. In return for rent and a small amount of equity, the incubators provide sponsorship and promotion, which might otherwise be unavailable to small firms. Examples of incubators are the Australian Technology Park, a Sydney-based collaboration between the University of New South Wales, the University of Technology and Sydney University. Another is the Playford Centre in South Australia, which is sponsored by the South Australian Government, Microsoft, Oracle and EDS Australia. Since opening early in 1998, the Playford Centre has already assisted more than 50 South Australian–domiciled IT companies, including Camtech and Maxamine.

The venture capital sector today and beyond

The Australian Venture Capital Association (AVCAL) formed in April 1992, represents and promotes the venture capital industry in Australia. Its members come from the majority of funds managers, investor groups, lawyers, accountants, merchant bankers and others who are associated with the industry. AVCAL's charter aims to 'promote the Australian venture capital industry and encourage investment in growing business enterprises'. Its objectives include promotion of professional and ethical standards and the provision of a unified voice for the industry. AVCAL is actively involved in the production of PricewaterhouseCoopers' *Economic Impact of Venture Capital*—an annual survey publication which provides important information on the impact on small business and the Australian economy—and is a partner with Arthur Andersen conducting other annual surveys of venture capital activity in Australia.

Today the venture capital market has grown to well over 40 professional investment groups, which collectively manage hundreds of funds with, in aggregate, over $2.7 billion. By comparison, in 1993 seventeen investment managers controlled only $507 million (1993 Arthur Andersen/AVCAL survey of development capital; 1998 AVCAL venture capital survey). The growth of venture capital has been enhanced by regular media reports highlighting the impressive growth and profit levels often experienced following investment. In the 1990s, companies backed by venture capital have significantly outperformed both the economy and the top 100 ASX-listed stocks, in terms of sales, profits, exports and employment growth.

Figure 1 indicates the significant influences which venture capital funding has on the overall growth and development of companies that receive investment.

Although expansion capital and management buy-ins/buy-outs still account for over 80 per cent of venture capital investment activity, the proportion of investments in seed, startup and early expansion is slowly increasing, largely due to encouragement

Figure 1

Comparison of growth data: VC-backed companies and top 100 ASX companies, 1992–96

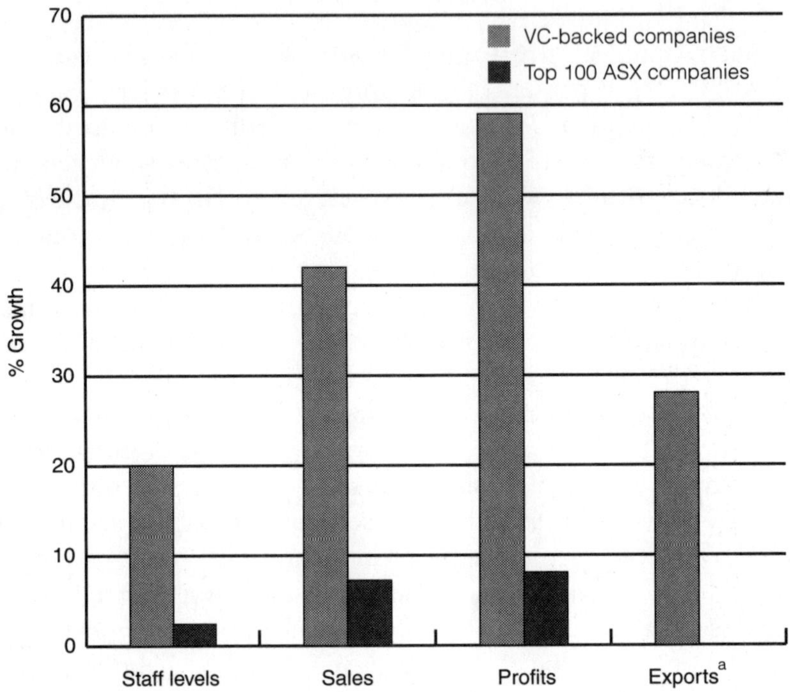

Note: [a] Top 100 companies data n/a
Source: *The Economic Impact of Venture Capital*, Coopers & Lybrand Economics Survey, 1997

from the government through the IIF program. As has been the case for most of the 1990s, manufacturing and technology firms are the largest recipients of venture capital, and in terms of geography New South Wales and Victoria receive over 60 per cent of the capital awarded. (*AVC Journal*, September 1999).

Venture capital investment is currently at record levels. The most recent Australian Venture Capital Association survey indicates that, at June 1998, over $1.7 billion was invested in 221 businesses, with 50 new businesses being the beneficiaries of new funding in the 1997/98 year. These beneficiaries are spread over many sectors.

Table 11

Breakdown of venture investment by industry and region

	Number of deals		Value of deals	
Industry	*Number*	*% Total*	*Value $m*	*% Total*
Agribusiness	15	4.73	35.91	5.27
Communications	25	7.89	30.18	4.43
Construction/housing	7	2.21	6.00	0.88
Distribution	10	3.15	21.49	3.15
Environment	6	1.89	2.76	0.40
Food/beverages	6	1.89	25.48	3.74
Health/bioscience	30	9.46	30.33	4.45
Information technology/software	55	17.35	61.01	8.95
Manufacturing—consumer	7	2.21	21.94	3.22
Manufacturing—industrial	39	12.30	239.45	35.14
Media/entertainment	14	4.42	42.23	6.20
Resources/mining	30	9.46	53.96	7.92
Retailing	7	2.21	8.46	1.24
Services—business	32	10.09	42.80	6.28
Services—consumer	7	2.21	11.73	1.72
Technology	10	3.15	16.24	2.38
Tourism/leisure	17	5.36	31.54	4.63
Total	**317**	**100.00**	**681.51**	**100.00**
Region				
New South Wales	115	36.30	213.35	31.30
Victoria	81	25.60	263.95	38.70
New Zealand	16	5.00	42.80	6.30
Queensland	17	5.40	35.39	5.20
Western Australia	52	16.40	58.43	8.60
South Australia	10	3.20	17.42	2.60
Tasmania	3	0.90	1.61	0.20
Australian Capital Territory	2	0.60	2.35	0.30
Northern Territory	2	0.60	7.62	1.10
Asia	2	0.60	0.06	0.00
Africa	1	0.30	7.80	1.10
North America	12	3.80	29.25	4.30
South America	1	0.30	1.00	0.10
Europe	3	0.90	0.48	0.10
Total	**317**	**100.00**	**681.51**	**100.00**

Source: *Australian Venture Capital Journal*/PricewaterhouseCoopers Survey, 1999

By far the most important thrust in the venture capital industry in the 1990s has come from the private sector. The major funds managers are listed in Table 12 (below). Many of these venture funds managers have developed large teams of full-time professionals and have been able to deliver attractive returns to investors.

Since the publication of Table 12 other capital raisings have been completed and announced. For example, Allen & Buckeridge have commenced a new technology fund targeting

Table 12

Australian venture capital firms, 1999

Top 25 fund managers and listed firms	*Capital ($m)*	*Top 25 private and captive firms*	*Capital ($m)*
AMP Business Development Funds	343	AMP Asset Management – Resources	900
Macquare Direct Investment	311	AMP Life	312
Deutsche Asset Management	291	UBS Capital	150
Rothschild Arrow Private Equity	226	AMP Asset Management NZ (NZ$)	110
Catalyst Investment Managers	185	Emerald Capital (NZ$)	100
BCR Asset Management	155	RMB Australia	100
Australian Mezzanine Investments	133.7	Lombard Group (NZ$)	100
Westpac Development Capital	125	Leyshon Group	80
Hambro-Grantham Management	115	Aboriginal & Torres Strait Islander CDC	64.1
AusAsean Management	110.2	Nomura/JAFCO Investment	60
GS Private Equity	103	Oceania & Eastern Group (NZ$)	55
Gresham Private Equity	102.5	Citicorp Equity Capital	50
Advent Management Group	100	National Australia Investment Capital	44
Lion Selection Group	100	Direct Capital Private Equity (NZ$)	35
Allen & Buckeridge	87	Resource Finance Corporation	35
Macquarie Technology Funds	78.3	Acma Australia	30
Development Capital of Australia	65	Australian Technology Group	30
CVC Investment Managers	62	Fairgill Investments	25.5
Technology Venture Partners	60	Flinders Capital	22.5
Pacific Equity Partners	50	Nepean Capital Partners	20
Gresham Rabo Management	49	Salisbury Group (NZ$)	20
Australasian Media & Communications	47.5	Accord Capital Investors	16
Greenchip Funds Management	47	Manufactured Construction Systems	9
AMWIN Management	41.2	Loftus Capital Partners	8
Coates Myer & Co.	41.2	Mercantile Mutual Investment Management	7
Total	**3028.6**	**Total**	**2383.1**

Source: *Australian Venture Capital Journal*, October 1999

$150 million, Gresham Partners closed a listed technology fund with about $70 million, and Australian Mezzanine has launched a $400 million management buy-out fund in partnership with the Castle Harlan group of New York.

Further evidence of the increasing interest in and depth of the Australian venture capital sector is the emergence of 'business angel' networks. As noted earlier, an 'angel' is typically a wealthy businessperson who, with other such individuals, may provide seed capital to young entrepreneurs with good ideas and emerging companies. These angels may provide more than just money, lending their own experience to assist entrepreneurs to develop their business models. Networks of angels are likely to invest in early-stage efforts before a venture capital company provides funding. Table 13 gives a list of networks.

Table 13

Australia's established 'business angel' networks

Network	*Territory*	*Investors*	*Investment range*	*Phone*	*Internet WWW*
Australian Business Angels	National	600	\$100k–\$1m	13 26 96	abol.net/abl/angels
BizEquity	Qld, NSW, Vic, WA	300+	\$50k–\$2.5m	07 5591 9531	bizequity.com.au
Business Angels	Vic	<500	\$25k–\$1m	03 9826 6800	businessangels.com.au
Corporation Builders	Qld, NSW, Vic, WA, Asia, Nth America, NZ	120	\$100k–\$50m	1800 807 0510	corpbuilders.com.au
Enterprise Market (ASX)	National	Goal: > 1000	Up to \$50m	03 9617 8676	asx.com.au/em
Entrex	Aust, Asia, Europe, USA	800	\$50k–\$5m+	08 9322 1155	entrex.com.au
VECCI	National	420	\$50k–\$2m	1800 671 689	n/a
TINSHED Angels	National/ international	18+	\$50k–\$2m	02 9211 2911	www.tinshed.com
East Coast Angels	East coast Australia	20–40	\$100k–\$1.5m	02 9221 8015	n/a

Source: AVCAL, www.avcal.com.au

Future directions

The next five years should see several trends occurring in the venture capital industry.

Superannuation funds will become a larger source of capital, with expectations that their allocations to the venture capital asset class will rise from the current levels of less than 2 per cent to not less than 5 per cent.

Increased specialisation of venture capital funds will occur as competition intensifies and venture capitalists manage more funds. This specialisation will emerge by stage of investment and by investee industry. For example, we will see specialist managers in early-stage internet funds, expansion-stage biotech funds, management buy-out (MBO) manufacturing funds, and so on.

More overseas capital will find its way into the Australian private capital markets, particularly from the United States. This will accelerate now that the Federal Government has embraced the Ralph Committee's recommendation that it remove capital gains tax presently preventing the world's largest suppliers of venture capital—the exempt US pension funds—from investing in Australian venture capital funds. For years prior to the formation of the Ralph Committee, AVCAL had lobbied intensively for the removal of this impediment. AVCAL's efforts in 1999 were professionally assisted by good work from the financial services firm, Deloittes. Important messages along the same lines were delivered by others, such as Peter Wills early in 1999, in a report to the Federal Government titled *The Health and Medical Research Strategic Review*. The report concluded that the venture capital Australia needed to match its intellectual capital would only be forthcoming if the capital gains tax laws were overhauled.

An increase in investments in startup and seed capital will occur as a result of the government's Innovation Investment Fund. This 'kickstart' will show high profit results from technology investing and will lead to larger private sector activity in this end of the business.

A rapid emergence of dedicated private equity specialists will occur within the advisory firms and intermediaries. For example, the large legal and accounting firms and the investment banks will all boast people and resources dedicated to the private capital deal flow, consulting and transaction business.

Increasing globalisation of the industry will ensue, with Australian venture-backed companies actively competing in world markets, including the capital markets of Asia, Europe and the United States. In turn, venture fund managers will need to be international in their reach and capacity. They will need to be able to rapidly complete due diligence and analysis of technologies and markets outside Australia. This need for active partners and alliances will manifest itself in mergers of fund managers and new entrants from the United States and elsewhere. All of this will be good for the industry as it increases in sophistication and depth.

The provision of private capital is likely to grow from the present level of around $700 million per annum to not less than $2 billion per annum within the next five year period, with at least half of this amount being invested in the management buy-out segment.

Along with these trends, the emergence of a specialised class of venture fund managers mandated by Australian and overseas institutional superannuation funds will significantly influence the future development of the venture capital industry. As the strategy and operations of Australian Mezzanine Investments have been shaped by our anticipation and belief in this likely pattern of development, I have chosen to end this book with a brief account of AMIL's evolution and its results to date.

a profile of the australian mezzanine investments group

Australian Mezzanine Investments Pty Limited (AMIL) was established in 1987 to focus on institutional funds management in the private capital business. It is the leading independently owned Australian private equity funds management group.

AMIL's first fund, the Australian Mezzanine Investments Trust (AMIT), was formed in 1988 as one of Australia's pioneering institutionally funded venture capital funds, with a broad private equity mandate. It invested some $30 million in nine companies across a number of domestic and international industry sectors.

Our No. 2 Trust was capitalised at $50 million and was launched in 1993. Its mandate was more closely focused on internationally competitive companies experiencing export-led growth, as well as buy-outs. The average size of investments was increased in order to target a portfolio size of ten investments at any one time.

In 1997 the Australian Mezzanine Investments No. 3 Trust closed oversubscribed at $82 million, with a similar mandate to that of the second fund.

The investors represented in the three Trusts include the superannuation funds of leading Australian public companies, State and Federal government authorities, industry superannuation funds and some successful venture capital entrepreneurs reinvesting profits in the next generation via Australian Mezzanine. These investors include:

- BHP Superannuation
- BNP Investment Management (Australia) Limited
- Commonwealth Superannuation Scheme Board
- CRA Group Staff Superannuation Funds/Comalco Employees Provident Fund
- Deutsche Asset Management Limited
- Funds SA
- KFT Investments Pty Ltd (Mr George Kepper)
- Labour Union Co-operative Retirement Fund
- Macquarie Alternative Investment Trust
- PostSuper Pty Ltd (Australia Post)
- Provident and Pensions Holdings Pty Ltd (Shell)
- Public Sector Superannuation Board
- Reserve Bank Officers' Superannuation Fund
- Retail Employees Superannuation Trust Pty Limited
- Stevedoring Employees Retirement Fund Pty Limited
- Superannuation Trust of Australia
- SZ Australia Investors Pty Ltd (Sam Zell group, Chicago)
- Tertiary Education Super Scheme
- Victorian Superannuation Board
- Westscheme Pty Ltd.

The professional-staff team at AMIL has expanded progressively to provide coverage of the growing portfolio with a strong network of industry contacts and to ensure a flow of quality investment opportunities. The professional team now numbers eight.

It has been a deliberate strategy of the AMIL group to develop an international network of private equity co-investors who can add value to Australian companies expanding into their regions. Co-investors from Asia and the United States have successfully assisted a number of AMIL portfolio companies with their offshore expansion and with their access to offshore capital markets.

A fourth fund, the AMWIN Innovation Fund, was established in 1998 as a joint venture among three parties: the Federal Government, the Walden International Investment Group of San Francisco, and AMIL. Formed as a licensee under the Innovation Investment Fund program of the Federal Government, AMWIN is a $42 million fund dedicated to investment in new technology companies at an early stage in their development.

AMWIN's first investment was in the then fledgling Melbourne-based internet search engine company, LookSmart Inc. LookSmart recently listed on the NASDAQ exchange and by November 1999 enjoyed a market capitalisation of almost A$5billion, demonstrating that it is indeed possible for an innovative, technology-driven Australian company to make it on a global basis.

AMIL's private sector partner in AMWIN, Walden, has been pre-eminent in its ability to bring early-stage companies from 'offshore' into the US product and capital markets. With established offices in Hong Kong, Singapore, Taipei, Israel and now Sydney, Walden brings valuable resources to complement AMIL's team.

Late in 1999 the founders of the AMIL group agreed to sell a 50 per cent interest to the successful New York–based private equity firm, Castle Harlan Inc. Castle Harlan has specialised in the management buy-out business, having completed over $US3 billion worth of such transactions in the US. It has now extended its activities into the Australasian region through this new partnership, which is called Castle Harlan Australian Mezzanine Partners (CHAMP). The partnership will continue to expand across all segments of the private equity business, in early-stage, expansion-stage and management buy-out investments.

The first fund launched by CHAMP is a A$400 million management buy-out fund. The investors in this fund are primarily investors from Castle Harlan's existing partnerships in the United States and investors from AMIL's existing investors in its funds in Australia.

This fund will be dedicated to management buy-out transactions (MBOs) in Australasia targeting 'middle market' sized companies, that is, companies whose revenues range between $75 million and $400 million per annum.

The founding partners of Castle Harlan Inc., John Castle and Leonard Harlan, first met at Donaldson Lufkin & Jenrette (DLJ) when they were among that famous merchant bank's earliest partners. John Castle went on to become the Chief Executive of DLJ prior to successfully selling the firm to the Equitable Life Insurance group.

John and Leonard teamed up in 1987 to launch their first dedicated MBO fund and now have more than A$1.5 billion under management. Their second fund is the top performing 1992 vintage MBO fund in the US, having achieved an internal rate of return in excess of 70 per cent.

John Castle and Leonard Harlan consistently pursued the objective of growing the companies in which they invest by empowering the management of those companies and by nurturing their growth plans with funding and management resources. This simple but fundamental business philosophy is one shared by AMIL.

The performance of venture capital funds is measured in terms of the internal rates of return (or compound annual growth rates) achieved by the funds over the term of their life. Institutional investors will normally expect the venture funds to exceed returns available in the public equities markets by a margin of at least 5 per cent per annum. This margin is required by the investors to compensate for the higher risks and reduced liquidity inherent in venture capital portfolios.

The AMIT funds have achieved the IRR results shown in Table 14, gross of management fees.

Table 14

Fund	Fund size ($m)	Fund IRR (%)	Years
AMIT No. 1	30	17.7	1988–98
AMIT No. 2	50	28.8	1993–99
AMIT No. 3	82	59.4	1997–99
MBOs[a]		87.3	1991–99

Note: [a] Represents the six management buy-out transactions completed by the various funds

These results were achieved in a portfolio of companies in the following sectors: information technology, specialty retailing, education services, superalloy manufacturing, biometrics, furniture supply, animal feed supplements, tourism, fast-ferry manufacturing, wine, software, internet search engine businesses, medical and health services, post-production audio equipment, mortgage origination, and other specialty manufacturing.

Further information regarding AMIL personnel and the portfolio companies may be obtained from our website at <www.amil.com>.

appendix

Australia's Co-operative Research Centres

Manufacturing technology
Advanced Composite Structures
Maritime Engineering
Materials Welding and Joining
Polymers
Molecular Engineering and Technology: Sensing and Diagnostic Technologies
Industrial Plant Biopolymers
Intelligent Manufacturing Systems and Technologies
Alloy and Solidification Technology
International Food Manufacture and Packaging Science

Information and communication technology
Robust and Adaptive Systems

Distributed Systems Technology
Photonics
Sensor Signal and Information Processing
Broadband Telecommunications and Networking
Advanced Computational Systems
Research Data Network
Satellite Systems

Mining and energy
Mining Technology and Equipment
Extractive Metallurgy
Petroleum
Hydrometallurgy
Mineral Exploration Technologies
New Technologies for Power Generation from Low-Rank Coal
Geodynamics
Landscape Evolution and Mineral Exploration
Black Coal Utilisation
Renewable Energy

Agriculture and related industries
Plant Science
Tropical Pest Management
Sustainable Production Forestry
Legumes in Mediterranean Agriculture
Tropical Plant Pathology
Hardwood Fibre and Paper Science
Viticulture
Premium Quality Wool
Cattle and Beef Industry (Meat Quality)
Aquaculture
Sustainable Cotton Production
Food Industry Innovation
Sustainable Sugar Production
Quality Wheat Products and Processes
Molecular Plant Breeding
Sustainable Rice Production

Environment
Waste Management and Pollution Control

Soil and Land Management
Antarctica and the Southern Ocean
Catchment Hydrology
Biological Control of Vertebrate Pest Populations
Ecologically Sustainable Development of the Great Barrier Reef
Freshwater Ecology
Southern Hemisphere Meteorology
Tropical Rainforest Ecology and Management
Sustainable Development of Tropical Savannas
Conservation and Management of Marsupials
Water Quality and Treatment
Weed Management Systems
Sustainable Tourism

Medical science and technology
Tissue Growth and Repair
Cellular Growth Factors
Eye Research and Technology
Biopharmaceutical Research
Cochlear Implant, Speech and Hearing Research
Cardiac Technology
Vaccine Technology
Diagnostic Technologies
Aboriginal and Tropical Health
Discovery of Genes for Common Human Diseases

index